TRUE CRIME QUIZ BOOK

CHRIS ALAN

ΛL
AD LIB

First published in the UK in 2023 by Ad Lib Publishers Ltd
15 Church Road
London SW13 9HE
www.adlibpublishers.com

Text © Ad Lib Publishers Ltd

Paperback ISBN 9781802471861

A CIP catalogue record for this book is available from the British Library.

Printed in the UK
10 9 8 7 6 5 4 3 2 1

MIX
Paper | Supporting
responsible forestry
FSC
www.fsc.org
FSC® C018072

CONTENTS

INTRODUCTION

Any hardened crook knows that the best way to respond to a question is with a firmly-set poker face and a stern 'no comment', but over the next [198] pages, we'd like you to dig deep into your true-crime knowledge and start coming up with some answers!

Challenge your friends, give the grey matter a workout, or use this book to inspire your next quiz night. And don't worry if your memory has suddenly gone a little hazy – you'll find loads of trivia to kick start your own investigations into the fascinating world of true crime, and the grisly murders, unsolved mysteries and underworld legends that have gripped the world for generations.

KILLERS

Nothing piques our morbid curiosity quite like the crime of murder, but perhaps there's something more at play than plain old rubbernecking – could it be that our grim fascination stems from some ancestral desire to arm ourselves against the predator? Ultimately, even that innate instinct is most likely futile. If history – and our first batch of ten quizzes – can teach us anything, it's that all too often, killers are hiding right there in plain sight.

Quiz 1 – Serial Killers

Serial killers are a breed apart – be they calculating, brazen or tormented, their cruelty seems to defy human nature. Little wonder, then, that we resort to language like 'beast' or 'monster' to describe their demented personalities. Dive into this trivia round to see how much you know about serial killers through the ages.

1. Murderer Danny Rolling slaughtered five students over a bloody four days in August 1990, and his spree went on to inspire the hit horror franchise *Scream*. What nickname did the press give Rolling, taken from the Florida city where the murders took place?

2. Staying with Florida, what is the name of the Florida sex worker executed in October 2002 for shooting seven men to death between 1989–90?

3. 'Angel of Death' nurse Beverley Allitt received thirteen life sentences for bringing terror to a children's ward in 1991, murdering four kids, attempting to murder three more and causing grievous bodily harm to another six. In what English county was the now derelict hospital where the crimes took place?

   a) Northumberland
   b) Lincolnshire
   c) North Yorkshire

4. It's said that some 300–400 child murders can be attributed to the 'Ogress of Reading' Amelia Dyer, making her a likely candidate for the most prolific serial killer in British history. Dyer took cash to adopt unwanted kids before strangling them to death, but in what century did her crimes take place?

   a) Sixteenth century
   b) Seventeenth century
   c) Nineteenth century

5. Anagram: rearrange 'Admonish Ralph' for the name of another highly prolific British serial killer with a medical bent.

6. What was one nickname given to the charismatic serial killer and fraudster Charles Sobhraj, who terrorised the south-east Asian hippy trail in the 1970s? The moniker was also the title of a BBC/ Netflix series starring Jenna Louise Coleman as Sobhraj's girlfriend.

7. Which infamous American kidnapper, murderer and rapist twice managed to escape custody before his execution by electric chair in 1989 for killing thirty women?

8. Police interviewed the Yorkshire Ripper, Peter Sutcliffe, nine times before his arrest following a routine traffic stop led to him being charged with murder – in which year?

   a) 1975
   b) 1981
   c) 1984

9. Fred and Rose West's garden at 25 Cromwell Street, Gloucester, yielded its first grim discovery just a day after the couple's arrest in February 1994, but whose remains were found buried and, for a bonus point, how was the victim known to the killer couple?

10. Nineteeth-century murderer Manuel Blanco Romasanta was said to be Spain's first serial killer. He confessed to thirteen murders and was convicted of nine – but denied responsibility on the grounds that a curse had turned him into which mythical creature?

    a) A werewolf
    b) A vampire
    c) El Coco

ANSWERS

1. The Gainesville Ripper.

2. Aileen Wuornos.

3. b)   Lincolnshire.

4. c)   Nineteenth century.

5. Harold Shipman.

6. The Serpent.

7. Ted Bundy.

8. b)   1981.

9. Heather West – she was their daughter.

10. a)   Werewolf. Romasanta became known as the 'Werewolf of Allariz'. But he had a second nickname, 'the Tallowman', for rendering his victims' fat to make soap.

Quiz 2 – Serial Killers and Mass Murderers

Match these killers to the locations forever associated with their heinous crimes listed below.

1. Ronald DeFeo Jr

2. Derrick Todd Lee

3. Ronald Jebson

4. Steve Wright

5. Gary Ridgway

6. Jeremy Bamber

7. Thierry Paulin

8. John Christie

9. Dennis Nilsen

10. Adam Lanza

a) Suffolk

b) White House Farm

c) Amityville

d) Muswell Hill

e) Sandy Hook

f) Rillington Place

g) Epping Forest

h) Green River, Washington

i) Montmartre

j) Baton Rouge

ANSWERS

1. c) The ghost stories may have been debunked, but the horror was undeniably real: DeFeo murdered his parents and siblings at the family home on Ocean Avenue, Amityville.

2. j) Lee was convicted of murdering two women in Baton Rouge and linked by DNA to another five killings.

3. g) Susan Blatchford and Gary Hanlon – the so-called 'Babes in the Wood' – were raped and murdered by Jebson in a copse on the edge of Epping Forest.

4. a) Steve Wright, AKA The Suffolk Strangler.

5. h) The mass murderer's first victims were found dumped in or near Green River.

6. b) Bamber was convicted of murdering his parents, adopted sister and her sons at the farm – a crime he denies to this day.

7. i) Paulin terrorised Paris's eighteenth *arrondissement* (district) in the 1980s, eventually confessing to the murders of twenty-one elderly women.

8. f) The house of horrors at Rillington Place yielded six bodies. Christie is said to be responsible for eight murders, including that of his wife, Ethel.

9. d) Nilsen's later killings, all committed in the north London district, earned him the moniker the 'Muswell Hill Murderer'.

10. e) Lanza slaughtered twenty-six people in a mass shooting at Sandy Hook Elementary School in 2012.

Quiz 3 – Murderer Who's Who

Match each murderer to one of the killer profiles listed below.

1. Joseph DeAngelo – the Golden State Killer

2. Stephen Port – the Grindr Killer

3. Dennis Rader – the BTK (Blind, Torture, Kill) Killer

4. Levi Bellfield

5. Barry Prudom – the Phantom of the Forest

6. Robert Hansen

7. Chester Turner

8. Benjamin Field

9. John Wayne Gacy Jr

10. Colin Norris

a) This balding serial killer wore a blond wig to cover up his hair loss and boost his confidence when he met his unsuspecting victims. He grew up in east London and tried his hand in art college before training as a chef. He worked in the catering team at a Stagecoach bus depot in West Ham where he made a brief appearance on *Celebrity MasterChef* helping the stars make meatballs.

b) This triple killer grew up in Leeds and trained as an electrician after leaving school before working on oil rigs. His efforts to join the SAS reserves failed at the last hurdle when he flunked the final test, however he maintained an interest in guns and the military and illegally carried a Beretta pistol. His knowledge of survival skills enabled him to evade capture for over two weeks amid what was at the time the biggest manhunt in British history.

c) After a twenty-two-month naval career during the Vietnam War, he gained a university degree in criminal justice and went on to become a police officer. His crime-fighting days were shortlived: in 1979, after six years in the force, he was sacked for shoplifting, and his time in the police also coincided with his first wave of break-ins, murders and rapes.

d) This shy loner grew up in Iowa and worked in the family bakery business. Suffering with a stutter and severe acne, he struggled to form relationships and was often bullied. He had a brief spell in the army where he became a skilled marksman. He later married and moved to Anchorage where he set up his own bakery and honed his skills as a hunter – skills he put to use in the abduction, rape and murder of multiple young women.

e) As a youth, he had a brief spell working as a mortuary attendant, but quit after climbing into a coffin to caress a dead body. He took a job with a shoe company before running a chain of KFC restaurants. His life unravelled after he was jailed for sodomy but as a model prisoner he was released early from his ten-year sentence. He settled near Chicago where he was known as a friendly guy who loved dressing as his alter ego – Pogo the Clown – to entertain kids.

f) This monster grew up in south-west London with his two brothers and two sisters, and was just ten when he lost his dad to leukaemia. He worked as a bouncer in various clubs and bars before changing jobs to become a wheel clamper and fathered eleven children with five different girlfriends.

g) Worked as a travel agent after college, but the job wasn't for him and he went into nursing. He disliked working with elderly patients and longed for the excitement of the A&E department. He's said to have killed his own cat with a lethal dose of insulin – practice for what would come later.

h) This wannabe poet was the son of a Baptist minister and was an avid reader as a child. He gained a degree in English literature and served as a church warden. He exchanged poems with his elderly victim and lover – and brazenly delivered the eulogy at his funeral.

i) He moved to LA at five years old and, after dropping out of high school at seventeen, worked as a cook and delivery guy for

Domino's pizza – he was still working for the fast-food chain when he committed his first murder. Despite multiple arrests for lewd conduct, indecent exposure and assault, it took police sixteen years to bring him to justice, by which time he had killed fourteen people.

j) As a kid, this multiple murderer killed stray cats and dogs for kicks and harboured violent fantasies about torturing women. He had a brief spell in the US airforce before getting married, later completing a degree in administration of justice. He settled on a job as a dogcatcher and maintained his guise as an innocent family man, church council president and scout leader for two decades before being brought to justice.

ANSWERS

1. c)

2. a)

3. j)

4. f)

5. b)

6. d)

7. i)

8. h)

9. e)

10. g)

Quiz 4 – International Serial Killers and Multiple Murderers – Whodunnit?

Evil truly lurks in every corner of the world. Match each of these killer profiles to a name from the list below.

1. Former teacher who murdered at least fifty-two in RUSSIA, even eating some of his victims, in a killing spree which lasted over a decade. He was able to keep killing for so long partly because Soviet authorities refused to believe serial murder was possible under communism. He was convicted in 1992 and executed with a single gunshot to the head.

2. Tortured, raped and mutilated over 190 boys and young men in 1990s' COLOMBIA. He posed as a monk to lure his victims, mostly street kids, promising drinks or cash. He was jailed for 1,853 years. Under Colombian law imprisonment is limited to forty years – and he got another eighteen years knocked off for helping police find his victims' corpses.

3. CHINA'S most prolific serial killer, he committed sixty-seven murders and twenty-three rapes between 2000–03. He would sneak into his victims' homes and batter them with improvised weapons like axes, hammers and shovels. He was executed by firing squad in 2004.

4. He killed thirty-seven women and girls in UKRAINE and the Soviet Union, using his job as a police investigator to throw detectives off the tracks and evading detection for twenty-five years. Several innocent men were wrongfully convicted of his crimes, with one even committing suicide. He was jailed for life in 2008 and died in prison a decade later.

5. He terrorised a suburb of Tokyo, JAPAN, between 1988–9, murdering four girls and dismembering their bodies before drinking blood from some of the parts and keeping others as grim trophies. He was arrested in 1989 and sentenced to death at the culmination of a seven-year trial. He was hanged in 2008.

6. He served an early life sentence for murdering a sex worker in his native AUSTRIA but saw the light and was released on parole in 1990, becoming a literary celebrity off the back of his bestselling prison memoir. He was far from reformed, however, and carried

out a string of murders in Austria and the USA, where he was finally arrested. Following his extradition, he was jailed for life but hanged himself in prison.

7. Stabbed his own mother and father to death in Mestre, ITALY, in 1981 and was locked up in a psychiatric hospital. He escaped after five years and went on the run in France, where he killed five more times over the next nine months. He was caught in 1988 after returning to his home town and died in jail, suffocating himself with a plastic bag.

8. Known as the 'Monster of Caracal'. He was jailed for thirty years in 2022 after police found the remains of two missing female hitchhikers in a barrel at his home in ROMANIA.

9. His farm became the largest crime scene in CANADA's history after police found the remains or DNA of thirty-three women among the pigsties. He was charged with twenty-six murders and convicted of six in 2007 – but reportedly confessed to killing forty-nine, lamenting that he wished he'd killed one more to make a round fifty.

10. Another cannibal serial killer, he terrorised the Ruhr region of GERMANY for two decades, claiming he ate his victims to save cash, as meat was expensive. He was finally snared in 1976 after clogging a neighbour's shared drain with one victim's entrails. Police found more body parts in his fridge and a severed hand cooking on the stove.

a) Serhiy Tkach

b) Luis Alfredo Garavito

c) Roberto Succo

d) Gheorghe Dinca

e) Andrei Chikatilo

f) Joachim Kroll

g) Jack Unterweger

h) Robert Pickton

i) Yang Xinhai

j) Tsutomu Miyazaki

ANSWERS

1. e)

2. b)

3. i)

4. a)

5. j)

6. g)

7. c)

8. d)

9. h)

10. f)

Quiz 5 – Killer Cannibals

Sink your teeth into this trivia round on some of world's grisliest killers.

1. Who did Spanish cannibal Alberto Sánchez Gómez share his mother's body parts with after strangling her to death in Madrid in 2019?

    a) His father
    b) The postman
    c) His dog

2. What nickname is serial killer Stephen Griffiths – who murdered three women in Bradford – better known by, thanks to the weapon he used to kill one of his victims?

3. What did toothless Russian cannibal Eduard Seleznev do to one of his victims in order to consume him?

    a) Turned him into a smoothie
    b) Made soup out of him
    c) Baked him in a pie

4. Mexican cocaine kingpin Heriberto Lazcano reportedly enjoyed cooking his victims' buttocks in lemon and eating them in tamales. Which notoriously bloodthirsty cartel did he head up before he was shot dead by Mexican naval marines in 2012?

5. What is the real name of the so-called 'Milwaukee Cannibal', one of the most famous serial killers in American history?

6. 'Rotenburg Cannibal' Armin Meiwes used an online forum to recruit a willing victim, Bernd Brandes, who actually agreed to be eaten. Which of Brandes' body parts did the two attempt to share before Meiwes stabbed him to death?

7. Which veteran rock'n'roll band once wrote a song about Japanese cannibal Issei Sagawa, who turned his Dutch girlfriend into a teriyaki after shooting her dead in Paris in 1981?

8. How was British killer cannibal Anthony Morley caught after killing and eating part of his victim's leg in Leeds in 2008?

    a) He walked into a takeaway covered in blood
    b) He announced his crime to a crowd at a bus stop
    c) He confessed during a live *This Morning* phone-in

9. What did New York cannibal Daniel Paul Rakowitz do with the surplus soup he made from boiling his roommate's brain?

    a) Froze it into meat lollipops
    b) Fed it to the homeless
    c) Served it up as gravy in a carvery

10. Similarly, how did Chinese cannibal Zhang Yongming dispose of some of his victims after preserving their eyes in wine bottles?

    a) Cooked stew for a poorly neighbour
    b) Made 'leather' bags and sold them on Etsy
    c) Sold them as ostrich meat in a local market

ANSWERS

1. c) His dog. He reportedly used a saw and knife to chop his mother into a thousand pieces, some of which were found in Tupperware containers.

2. The 'Crossbow Cannibal'. He reportedly told police he had eaten parts of one victim, Suzanne Blamires.

3. a) He used a blender to make meat smoothies.

4. Los Zetas.

5. Jeffrey Dahmer. He murdered seventeen young men, eating the biceps, heart, liver and pieces of thighs of some and preserving the severed heads and spray-painted skulls of many more.

6. Brandes' penis. Meiwes consumed the rest of the corpse over the following ten months. He was later convicted of murder and jailed for life.

7. The Rolling Stones' 'Too Much Blood' is about Sagawa. He largely escaped justice: after two years in prison awaiting trial he was declared unfit to stand and was deported to Japan. Authorities there ruled he was sane and a legal loophole allowed him to walk free.

8. a) He walked into the kebab shop in the early hours of the morning and asked the owners to call the police. He's serving life with a minimum thirty-year tariff.

9. b) He fed it to the homeless in Tompkins Square Park.

10. c) Sold them as ostrich meat.

Quiz 6 – Mass Shooters

A transatlantic trivia round covering some of the worst mass shootings in recent history.

1. In which part of the United Kingdom are handguns still permitted despite the commonly held belief that they were banned across the board in the wake of the 1996 Dunblane massacre?

2. Which troubled ex-footballer famously turned up in his dressing gown at the scene of a police stand-off with spree shooter Raoul Moat carrying a chicken, a fishing rod and some cans of lager?

3. Who was responsible for the 1987 'Hungerford Massacre' which left seventeen dead, including the killer and his mother, and fifteen injured?

4. How did spree killer Derrick Bird lure victims to his car in order to shoot them dead during his forty-five-mile rampage through Cumbria in June 2010?

    a) He asked them to tell him the time
    b) He offered them sweets
    c) He pretended he'd broken down

5. Which British coastal city was terrorised in 2021 by mass shooter Jake Davison, who went on a rampage with a pump action shotgun, killing five and wounding two more?

6. Name the Orlando nightspot where mass shooter Omar Mateen murdered forty-nine people in 2016, armed with a Sig Sauer rifle and a Glock pistol.

7. In 2017, which US city was the scene of the deadliest mass shooting in modern American history, with fifty-eight dead and hundreds more injured?

8. Which American gunmaker made legal history in 2022 when it became the first to be implicated in a mass shooting, reaching a $73-million settlement with the families of the dead in the Sandy Hook massacre?

   a) Browning
   b) Remington
   c) Smith & Wesson

9. Which El Paso supermarket was the scene of an anti-Latino attack in which shooter Patrick Crusius murdered twenty-three people with a Romanian-made WASR-10 semi-automatic rifle?

10. In which US state did the country's deadliest school shooting in history occur in April 2007?

ANSWERS

1. Northern Ireland.

2. Paul 'Gazza' Gascoigne.

3. Michael Ryan. He shot himself in the head during a stand-off with police.

4. a) He asked them the time. Bird killed twelve people and injured eleven before turning his gun on himself.

5. Plymouth. Davison held a shotgun licence but had his gun seized by police in December 2020 after he beat up a teenager. Cops deemed his risk to be low and returned it to him in July 2021, a month before his attack.

6. Pulse.

7. Las Vegas.

8. b) Remington. Shooter Adam Lanza was armed with an assault rifle made by Remington and killed twenty children and six adults before taking his own life.

9. Walmart.

10. Virginia. Undergrad student Seung-Hui Cho killed thirty-two people at the Virginia Polytechnic Institute and State University before shooting himself.

Quiz 7 – Killer Kids

The ultimate definition of innocence lost? Ten questions on kids who killed . . .

1. In which northwest city was eleven-year-old Rhys Jones shot and killed by stray bullets fired by sixteen-year-old gang member Sean Mercer in 2007?

2. Craig Mulligan was just thirteen when, alongside his stepdad John Cole and Logan's mum Angharad Williamson, he murdered five-year-old Logan Mwangi. Mulligan also helped his stepdad dispose of the victim's body – where was Logan found?

3. In April 2014, teacher Ann Maguire was knifed to death by one of her pupils, fifteen-year-old William Cornick, during class. What subject did she teach?

4. How many trials did it take to bring the killers of ten-year-old Damilola Taylor to justice?

   a) 3
   b) 4
   c) 7

5. What makeshift weapon was used to inflict the fatal wound on Damilola before he bled to death in a stairwell?

6. In 2015, sixteen-year-old Daniel Stroud fatally stabbed schoolmate Bailey Gwynne at a school in Aberdeen in a row that was said to have started over . . . what?

   a) A lost pencil sharpener
   b) Cheating in exams
   c) A biscuit

7. Lorraine Thorpe was fifteen when she became Britain's youngest female double-murderer, after she and accomplice Paul Clarke killed twice in 2009, beginning by torturing fellow street-drinker Rosalyn Hunt to death. How was Thorpe related to the duo's second victim?

8. Thorpe was superseded seven years later, when fourteen-year-old Kim Edwards teamed up with boyfriend Lucas Markham to knife her mother and sister to death as they slept. Which teen vampire romance movie did they watch after committing their crime, gifting the press a handy nickname for the murderous duo?

9. Another 'youngest' – Mary Bell remains Britain's youngest female killer after strangling to death two pre-school boys in 1968. What crime was she convicted of?

10. Which far right media commentator was criticised for seemingly linking the rape and murder of six-year-old Alesha MacPhail on the Isle of Bute in 2018 to Syrian refugees – before the killer was revealed as sixteen-year-old local boy Aaron Campbell?

ANSWERS

1. Liverpool.

2. In a river near the family home in Bridgend, South Wales. All three were found guilty of murder and jailed for life.

3. Spanish.

4. a) Three. Damilola died in 2000. Four youths were acquitted of murder in 2002. In 2006, gang-connected brothers Ricky and Danny Preddie were tried for manslaughter but the jury was unable to reach a verdict. They were tried again later the same year and found guilty. They were just thirteen and twelve years old when they killed Damilola.

5. A broken bottle.

6. c) A biscuit. Bailey had some and refused to share them with Stroud, who was later cleared of murder but convicted of culpable homicide and jailed for nine years.

7. The second victim was Lorraine's dad, Desmond Thorpe. Lorraine and Paul were convicted of the two murders and jailed in 2010.

8. *Twilight*. The pair became known in the press as the 'Twilight Killers'.

9. Manslaughter on the grounds of diminished responsibility. She was just ten years old when she committed her first murder – the day before her eleventh birthday – and committed the second two months later. She was released in 1980, granted lifelong anonymity and has lived under pseudonyms ever since.

10. Katie Hopkins. In the aftermath of the murder she tweeted two news articles – one concerning an increase in sex crimes in Argyll and Bute and another about Syrian refugees moving into the area.

Quiz 8 – Jack the Ripper

His reign of terror may have been short, but our fascination with his crimes endures to this day. Jack the Ripper gets a trivia round all to himself.

1. In a letter claiming to be from Jack the Ripper and sent to the chairman of a volunteer Whitechapel patrol group, which bodily organ did the killer say he had taken from one victim and eaten?

2. All but one of Jack the Ripper's victims had been mutilated with knife wounds causing horrific abdominal injuries – true or false?

3. Which bodily organ was missing from the corpse of Mary Jane Kelly, believed to be the last of the Ripper's victims?

4. Which celebrated impressionist artist has been named by some researchers as the true identity of Jack the Ripper?

5. The killer only became known as 'Jack the Ripper' thanks to a letter sent to a press agency after the first two murders, signed 'Yours truly, Jack the Ripper' – true or false?

6. Fourth victim Catherine Eddowes was released from a police station barely two hours before she was found murdered, having spent the evening locked up. Why had she been detained?

   a) She was caught soliciting for prostitution
   b) She had been found drunk
   c) For her own safety

7. The founder of which famous youth support charity, still active today, claimed to have met Ripper victim Elizabeth Stride and later used the murders to call for support for children's homes?

8. The Ripper murders took place in which year?

   a) 1888   b) 1890   c) 1901

9. Which member of the Royal family has fallen under suspicion of being Jack the Ripper?

10. Which police force investigated the murder of Catherine Eddowes?

ANSWERS

1. The letter came with half a human kidney. Whoever wrote it said they had eaten the other half.

2. True. Only Elizabeth Stride's abdomen was left intact, leading to suggestions her killer may have been disturbed in the act.

3. Her heart.

4. Walter Sickert.

5. True. Central News Agency received the missive and passed it on to the police, who duly released it in the wake of the double murder of Elizabeth Stride and Catherine Eddowes.

6. b) She'd been locked up for drunkenness but by midnight had sobered up enough to be released.

7. Dr Thomas Barnardo.

8. a) 1888.

9. Prince Albert Victor Christian Edward, grandson of Queen Victoria. The claims have been widely debunked.

10. City of London police. The other murders fell under the jurisdiction of the Met.

Quiz 9 – The Moors Murders

The Moors killers' shocking legacy never fails to horrify. See how much you know about this criminal couple in this trivia round.

1. What nationality was Ian Brady?

2. What was Brady's birth name?

   a) Ian Hindley
   b) Ian Gorbals
   c) Ian Stewart

3. How many child murders were the duo convicted of?

4. And how many did they eventually confess to in 1987?

5. What ruse would Hindley use as an excuse to drive some of the pair's young victims to Saddleworth Moor?

   a) She needed help looking for a lost glove
   b) There was a wild pony stuck in the mud
   c) She needed help putting out a grass fire

6. How were the two eventually caught?

   a) Ian Brady bragged about the murders at work
   b) They left Hindley's camera at one burial site
   c) They killed their final victim in front of Hindley's brother-in-law

7. Brady spent some twenty years of his time in prison translating classical texts into what?

8. Which female killer was Hindley said to have embarked on a romance with while the pair were incarcerated in Durham prison?

9. Which of the two Moors killers was the first to die in prison?

10. What is the name of the one child victim whose remains have never been found?

ANSWERS

1. Scottish.

2. c) Ian Stewart.

3. Three – John Kilbride, Lesley Ann Downey and Edward Evans. Brady was found guilty of all three, Hindley was convicted of murdering Downey and Evans.

4. Five – they later confessed to killing Pauline Reade and Keith Bennett.

5. a) The lost glove lie was used on Pauline Reade and John Kilbride.

6. c) David Smith – married to Hindley's sister Maureen – was present when Edward Evans was killed and, in fear of his own life, helped clear up after the axe murder. He called the police hours later.

7. Braille, for schools for the blind.

8. Rose West.

9. Myra Hindley – Brady survived her by almost fifteen years.

10. Keith Bennett.

Quiz 10 – Harold Shipman

It's Dr Death himself, up there among the most prolific serial killers in British history. Here's ten on Shipman.

1. How many patients is Shipman said to have killed?

   a) Around 75
   b) Around 120
   c) Around 250

2. How many murders was he actually convicted of?

   a) 9
   b) 15
   c) 33

3. What was his modus operandi?

4. What almost derailed his career in medicine just a year after he took up his first post as a GP?

   a) He was caught in a brothel
   b) He had an affair with a patient
   c) He got addicted to drugs

5. In which Manchester suburb did Shipman go on to establish his own GP practice?

6. Shipman's forgery of which document brought him to the attention of the police?

7. How many victims were exhumed in the course of the police inquiry?

   a) 8
   b) 12
   c) 23

8. In 2023, Britain's Advertising Standards Authority (ASA) censured a company for causing widespread offence by using Shipman's image to market . . . what?

9. In what year did Shipman hang himself in his cell at Wakefield prison?

   a) 2004
   b) 2008
   c) 2011

10. How was then home secretary David Blunkett said to have reacted to news of Shipman's demise?

   a) He blurted out 'Yes!' during Prime Minister's Question Time.
   b) He considered opening a bottle to celebrate.
   c) He danced on the table singing, 'Ding dong the beast is dead.'

ANSWERS

1. c) The generally accepted figure is around 250, but some have suggested he may have killed as many as 450.

2. b) Fifteen.

3. He injected his victims with morphine overdoses.

4. c) He got addicted to pethidine and was caught forging prescriptions.

5. Hyde.

6. A patient's will. It cut off Kathleen Grundy's family and left the eighty-one-year-old's £386,000 to Shipman. Police found his fingerprint on the fake document.

7. b) Twelve.

8. Life insurance. Complaints against the firm, DeadHappy, were upheld by the ASA. The company was told not to repeat the ads, which included the tagline, 'Because you never know who your doctor might be.'

9. a) 2004.

10. b) He has said publicly that he wondered if it was too soon to open a bottle and was criticised for sharing his thoughts.

ESPIONAGE AND TREACHERY

The complex web of spies, counterintelligence and betrayal spans history and international borders, and enemies of the state come in many different guises.

Quiz 11 – Spies, Traitors and Treason

Try and do better than 007 out of ten in this trivia round . . .

1. British embassy security guard David Smith was jailed for thirteen years in February 2023 after he was caught spying for Russia. Where was the embassy?

2. In 2018, which Middle Eastern country jailed British PhD student Matthew Hedges for life on accusations of spying for MI6, only to release him days later under a royal pardon?

3. American-born Nazi propagandist William Joyce was captured by British forces in Germany in 1945 and became the last person in the UK to be executed for high treason. By what nickname was he better known?

4. What year was capital punishment for high treason (as well as piracy, espionage and arson in royal docklands) finally abolished in the UK?

   a) 1990
   b) 1998
   c) 2001

5. Convicted of espionage in 1941 and sentenced to death by firing squad, what nationality was the last person to be executed at the Tower of London?

6. How was John Vassall, a British embassy worker stationed in Moscow, forcibly recruited to spy for the KGB, leading to an eighteen-year jail sentence?

   a) He was the victim of a honeytrap
   b) His daughter was taken hostage
   c) His bank account was frozen

7. Labour MP John Stonehouse was convicted of theft, fraud and deception after trying to fake his own disappearance in 1974, but he was also the subject of unproven accusations that he was a spy – for which Eastern bloc nation?

8. In 2023, Jaswant Singh Chail became the first person in over forty years to be convicted of a crime under the Treason Act after he was caught stalking the Queen with a crossbow. Which royal residence grounds was he arrested in?

9. How many years of his forty-two-year sentence for espionage did notorious cold war double-agent George Blake serve before escaping from Wormwood Scrubs in 1966 and fleeing to the Soviet Union?

   a) 1
   b) 5
   c) 13

10. MI5 agent Michael Bettany was locked up for twenty-three years in 1984 after photographing secret files and trying to pass them to the KGB. What language did he learn while in prison?

ANSWERS

1. Berlin.

2. United Arab Emirates.

3. Lord Haw-Haw.

4. b)   1998.

5. Josef Jakobs was German.

6. a)   He was honeytrapped into taking part in a gay orgy and blackmailed.

7. Czechoslovakia.

8. Windsor Castle.

9. b)   Five years. He spent the rest of his days in Moscow and was buried there with military honours on his death in 2020.

10. Russian.

CYBERCRIME AND WHISTLEBLOWERS

The nature of crime shifts with the ages and the digital realm has its fair share of crooks. A masterfully designed bit of computer code can extract millions of dollars from the unwary victim, and hackers can wreak havoc on the virtual infrastructures behind some of our biggest institutions.

Quiz 12 – Cybercrime and Whistleblowers

Answer this trivia ten on extraordinary leaks and hackers.

1. What message did Scottish hacker Gary McKinnon leave for dumbfounded IT experts as he trawled through NASA and US defence sites in 2001 looking for evidence of UFO cover-ups?

   a) 'Gary woz 'ere.'
   b) 'Your security is crap.'
   c) 'They walk among us.'

2. McKinnon was accused of hacking almost a hundred NASA and US military computers but his extradition to the States was blocked by home secretary Theresa May . . . on what medical grounds?

3. What is the name of the global hacker activist collective known for its high-profile cyber attacks on big business and governments?

4. The collective's members often identify themselves online wearing a stylised mask of which infamous British traitor – or rebel, depending on your politics?

5. Name the Australian journalist and founder of Wikileaks, currently being held in Belmarsh prison as he battles US efforts to extradite him on charges of publishing leaked documents.

6. In which London-based foreign embassy did the Wikileaks founder spend seven years after claiming political asylum – until it was revoked in 2019?

7. What is the name of the whistleblower and former US military intelligence analyst – who transitioned from male to female – jailed for an initial term of thirty-five years for disclosing secret military documents relating to Iraq and Afghanistan?

8. Which US-based global banking giant was targeted by Russian hackers in the mid-nineties in what is thought be the first virtual bank robbery, netting the crooks some ten million dollars before they were taken down by the FBI?

   a) Wells Fargo
   b) Bank of America
   c) Citibank

9. Which British institution was hit by the 'WannaCry' ransomware attack in May 2017, leading to the cancellation of 19,000 appointments and costing it ninety-two million pounds?

10. Hacker turned security expert Michael Calce called himself 'MafiaBoy' in 2000, when he took down Yahoo, Amazon, eBay, CNN and Dell in widely publicised attacks that caused a reported billion dollars of damage – yet he only got eight months of 'open custody' and a small fine when he was caught. Why?

ANSWERS

1. b) 'Your security is crap.'

2. He has Asperger's syndrome. McKinnon was never extradited, nor was he ever charged in the UK.

3. Anonymous.

4. Guy Fawkes.

5. Julian Assange.

6. Ecuadorian embassy.

7. Chelsea Manning, formerly Private Bradley Manning. Her sentence was commuted by President Obama and she was released in 2017.

8. c) Citibank.

9. The NHS.

10. He was a mere fifteen years old when he committed his crimes.

CELEBS GONE BAD?

Sometimes stars go off the rails and despite their status – or maybe because of it – some famous faces are just downright bad. From tax avoiders to killers, from sporting legends to supermodels, this section covers some dizzying falls from grace.

Quiz 13 – Celebrity Whodunnit

Match these celebrity jailbirds to the offence they were locked up for from the list below.

1. Boxer Mike Tyson

2. Shamed glam rocker Gary Glitter

3. Disgraced American football icon OJ Simpson

4. Eighties' pop icon George Michael

5. Rap mogul and Death Row Records supremo Suge Knight

6. Hollywood actor Wesley Snipes

7. 'Tiger King' Joe Exotic, AKA Joseph Maldonado-Passage

8. Singer and DJ Boy George

9. 'Wall of sound' music producer Phil Spector

10. Stand-up comedian and actor Tim Allen

a) Crashed his Range Rover into a shop while high on cannabis, earning him an eight-week sentence, of which he served a month.

b) Jailed for life with a minimum of nineteen years for shooting dead an actress he met in a bar. He died in prison after getting Covid-19.

c) Convicted in 2008 for wilful failure to file income tax returns. His appeal against conviction failed and he was jailed in 2010 for three years.

d) Locked up in December 2008 after a jury found him guilty of kidnapping, assault, armed robbery and burglary while in possession of a deadly weapon.

e) This serial fiend was caged for sixteen years in February 2015 for sexually abusing three schoolgirls. He was released after serving half his sentence only to be recalled a month later for breaching his licence conditions.

f) Falsely imprisoned a male escort with a pair of handcuffs and battered him with a metal chain as he escaped. He got fifteen months in prison.

g) Jailed for six years in March 1992 after being convicted of rape. Released in 1995 after serving three years.

h) Before finding fame, he was convicted in the late seventies of trafficking cocaine and spent two years in prison.

i) Pleaded no contest to voluntary manslaughter after causing the death of a man he ran over. Sentenced to twenty-eight years in October 2018.

j) Convicted of a murder-for-hire charge and jailed for twenty-two years in 2020. He had his sentence reduced by a year in 2022.

ANSWERS

1. g)

2. e)

3. d)

4. a)

5. i)

6. c)

7. j)

8. f)

9. b)

10. h)

Quiz 14 – Celebrity Trivia

1. In 1998 – long before he found fame as a TV chef – Gino D'Acampo was sentenced to two years in prison after breaking into the home of a famous pop singer to steal guitars and a platinum disc. It was the home of . . .

   a) Paul Weller   b) Paul McCartney   c) Paul Young

2. What crime did Fugees singer Lauryn Hill serve three months in prison for after being jailed in 2013?

3. Which serial-offender supermodel has been convicted of assault no less than four times?

4. In which city was Paul McCartney busted in in 1980 after jetting into the country with half a pound of marijuana in his baggage?

5. Which short-lived punk icon died of a heroin overdose in 1979 hours after being released from seven weeks of detox in New York's Rikers Island jail?

6. Name the sex worker famously arrested alongside actor Hugh Grant in LA in 1995 for 'lewd conduct'.

7. Which Texan Hollywood star recounted in his memoir, *Greenlights*, his 1999 arrest for breach of the peace while playing the bongos naked and stoned?

8. Iconic *EastEnders'* character 'Dirty' Den came to an apparent sticky end in 1989 when he was shot and collapsed in a canal. However, the actor who played him was himself convicted of shooting dead a taxi driver in a bungled robbery years before finding fame. What was the actor's name?

9. Back in 1970, Jane Fonda spent a night in the cells on suspicion of smuggling drugs after flying to Ohio. What in her luggage did police officers mistake for 'suspicious pills'?

   a) Smarties   b) Vitamins   c) Worming tablets

10. Paedophile weatherman Fred Talbot was famous for leaping across a map floating in Liverpool's Albert Dock during which TV show?

ANSWERS

1. c) Paul Young.

2. She failed to pay tax on two million dollars of earnings.

3. Naomi Campbell.

4. Tokyo. The Beatle spent nine days in the city's Narcotics Detention Centre before being deported. Wings' eleven-date tour was cancelled.

5. Sid Vicious.

6. Divine Brown.

7. Matthew McConaughey. He paid a $50 fine for creating a noise disturbance.

8. Leslie Grantham.

9. b) Vitamins. Fonda was released without charge the next day, but not before posing for an iconic mugshot with a defiant 'power to the people' fist.

10. *This Morning*.

TRUE CRIME ON THE SCREEN

The real-life antics of organised crooks, killers and con artists – and the cops who try to take them down – have made for unforgettable moments on film and TV, with some of the world's greatest directors offering an intoxicating peek beyond the curtain at the crimes, lives and characters behind the newspaper headlines.

Quiz 15 – Screen Time Trivia, US Edition

1. Which 1983 Brian De Palma gangster flick about the rise of a Cuban immigrant in Miami is a loose remake of a 1932 film of the same name which was in turn inspired by a notorious prohibition-era mob boss?

2. Which Hollywood legend played Harlem drug kingpin Frank Lucas – who infamously claimed to have smuggled heroin in the coffins of dead soldiers flown back from Vietnam – in Ridley Scott's biopic *American Gangster*?

3. Leonardo DiCaprio played which American fraudster and boiler-room scam artist in Martin Scorcese's darkly comic biopic, *The Wolf of Wall Street*? For a bonus point, who played the crook's second wife in what would prove to be a breakout role?

4. Sticking with Scorcese, *Goodfellas* was based on a non-fiction book, *Wiseguy*, chronicling the life of which Italian crime-family-associate-turned-FBI-informant?

   a) Harry Hill
   b) Henry Hill
   c) Hugo Hill

5. Double murderer and body snatcher Ed Gein is said to have inspired the serial killer in *Silence of the Lambs* who, like Gein, flays cadavers and wears their skins. But what is the name of the fictional character Agent Clarice Starling is tasked with catching?

6. Which 1997 Mike Newell mob flick stars Johnny Depp as real-life FBI agent Joseph D. Pistone, as he goes undercover to infiltrate the Bonanno crime family?

7. Anagram: Rearrange 'bandy indolence' for the name of a 1967 movie starring Faye Dunaway about the murderous exploits of a depression-era, bank-robbing criminal couple.

8. Which real-life actress and Manson family murder victim was played by Margot Robbie in Quentin Tarantino's *Once Upon a Time in Hollywood*?

9. What is the nationality of the conwoman who went by the name Anna Delvey and whose story was turned into the hit Netflix series *Inventing Anna*?

    a) German
    b) American
    c) Russian

10. The story of which infamous miscarriage of justice was told in another Netflix series, *When They See Us*?

    a) The 'Birmingham Six'
    b) The 'Central Park Five'
    c) The 'M25 Three'

ANSWERS

1. *Scarface.*

2. Denzel Washington.

3. Jordan Belfort and, bonus answer, Margot Robbie.

4. b)   Henry Hill.

5. Buffalo Bill.

6. *Donnie Brasco.*

7. *Bonnie and Clyde.*

8. Sharon Tate.

9. c)   Russian.

10. b)   The 'Central Park Five'.

Quiz 16 – Screen Time Trivia, UK Edition

1. Which late eighties' movie starring Phil Collins in the title role was based on the Great Train Robbery and spawned a hit for the Four Tops with the single 'Loco in Acapulco'?

2. Which East End gangster duo were played by a single actor – Tom Hardy – doubling up in the movie *Legend*? For a bonus point – in another movie, the same pair were played by real-life brothers from which eighties' pop band?

3. Staying with Hardy for a moment, which 2008 movie sees him get full frontal naked to play one of Britain's longest-serving and most notorious prisoners, who was denied release in a much-publicised parole hearing in 2023?

4. Who played Muswell Hill murderer Dennis Nilsen in ITV's 2020 drama, *Des*?

5. In which northern city would you find Lumb Lane, the former red-light district, whose sex workers inspired writer Kay Mellor's standout nineties' crime drama series *Band of Gold*?

6. In what country did Anne Darwin and husband John – who faked his own death in 2002 – plan to start a new life together, as depicted in 2022 drama series *The Thief, his Wife and The Canoe*? Was it:

   a) Brazil
   b) France
   c) Panama

7. Which Midlands city was home to the Peaky Blinders?

8. The failed 1962 plot to assassinate French President Charles de Gaulle inspired the opening scenes of which 1971 Frederick Forsyth novel, and a film of the same name released two years later?

9. Martin Clunes starred in two seasons of ITV series *Manhunt* as the Met police detective who brought serial killer Levi Bellfield and 'Night Stalker' Delroy Grant to justice. What is the officer's name?

   a) Colin Stagg
   b) Colin Sutton
   c) Colin Port

10. The unrelated murders of Keith Frogson and Chanel Taylor, which occurred just days apart in Nottinghamshire in 2004, inspired a 2022 BBC drama series set against the legacy of the miners' strikes and starring David Morrissey. What is the series called?

ANSWERS

1. *Buster.*

2. The Kray Twins. Bonus point: Spandau Ballet.

3. *Bronson.*

4. David Tennant.

5. Bradford.

6. c)   Panama.

7. Birmingham.

8. *The Day of the Jackal.*

9. b)   Colin Sutton.

10. *Sherwood.*

Quiz 17 – Famous Lines

Match these famous lines of dialogue to a movie from the list below.

1. 'It's as if Perry and I grew up in the same house. And one day he stood up and went out the back door, while I went out the front.'

2. 'I always wanted to be in the movies. When I was little, I thought for sure that one day, I could be a big, big star.'

3. 'I'm "funny" how? I mean, funny like I'm a clown, I amuse you? I make you laugh, I'm here to fuckin' amuse you? What do you mean "funny"? Funny how? How am I funny?'

4. 'I heard you paint houses.'

5. 'I'm a firm believer in karma and I think this situation was attracted into my life as a huge learning lesson for me to grow and expand as a spiritual human being.'

6. 'Take your shot, but make it your best. 'Cause I get up, I eat ya.'

7. 'Dear Dad, you always told me that an honest man has nothing to fear, so I'm trying my best not to be afraid.'

8. 'People don't realise that murderers do not come out in the dark with long teeth and saliva dripping off their chin. People don't realise that there are killers among them.'

9. 'If you let yourself be too scared then you let the bad guys take over the country, don't you? And then everybody gets scared.'

10. 'There's no such thing as truth. It's bullshit. Everyone has their own truth, and life just does whatever the fuck it wants.'

a) *The Irishman*

b) *Capote*

c) *Black Mass*

d) *Extremely Wicked, Shockingly Evil and Vile*

e) *Monster*

f) *I, Tonya*

g) *Bling Ring*

h) *JFK*

i) *Catch Me If You Can*

j) *Goodfellas*

ANSWERS

1. b) Philip Seymour Hoffman in the leading role as writer Truman Capote, documenting the 1959 murder of the Clutter family in Kansas.

2. e) That's Charlize Theron playing multiple murderer Aileen Wuornos.

3. j) It's wildcard Tommy DeVito, played by Joe Pesci, in *Goodfellas'* nerve-wracking nightclub scene.

4. a) Al Pacino's Jimmy Hoffa to hitman Frank Sheeran played by Robert DeNiro.

5. g) Emma Watson as Nicki, based on real life Bling Ringer Alexis Neiers.

6. c) It's Johnny Depp as sinister Boston mobster Whitey Bulger.

7. i) Leonard DiCaprio in the role of charming grifter Frank Abagnale Jr.

8. d) It's serial killer Ted Bundy channelled by Zac Efron.

9. h) Kevin Costner's Jim Garrison gets deep as he questions the narrative.

10. f) Figure skater Tonya Harding played by Margot Robbie.

WOMEN IN CRIME

From drug lords to serial killers to con artists, these fiendish females prove crime is anything but a man's world.

Quiz 18 – Women in Crime Trivia

1. How did the sentencing of thirty-eight-year-old Jemma Mitchell, jailed for life in 2022 for decapitating a friend and dumping her corpse in a suitcase, make British legal history?

2. What was the occupation of Mexican serial killer Juana Barraza, convicted of killing sixteen elderly women and suspected of being behind many more deaths?

   a) Wrestler
   b) Nurse
   c) Butcher

3. Which drug cartel was 'cocaine godmother' Griselda Blanco associated with?

4. How did Italian serial killer Leonarda Cianciulli cleanly dispose of her three victims' bodies before she was brought to justice in 1946?

5. What massive lie did conwoman and Australian wellness influencer Belle Gibson tell her legions of online followers to market her recipe book and app?

6. What controversial therapy for mental illness did Rose West's mother undergo while the infant Rose was still in her womb, leading some to suggest the future monster's serial killer psychology was forged even before birth?

7. What is the real name of the suspected British terrorist known as the 'White Widow', who is said to be behind four hundred deaths since becoming a jihadist and is the subject of an Interpol global arrest warrant?

8. Which dark moment in 2005 earned the White Widow her moniker?

9. Which 'Manson Family' member's name was adopted by a notoriously hard-partying British rock act who found fame in the mid-2000s?

10. In 2008, which Yorkshire town became the scene of a massive twenty-four-day search for missing nine-year-old Shannon Matthews, which was later revealed as a hoax orchestrated by her mum, Karen, in the hope of cashing in on a fifty-thousand-pound reward?

ANSWERS

1. It was the first in England and Wales to be televised.

2. a) She was a professional wrestler who went under the name 'La Dama del Silencio' ('The Lady of Silence'). She pretended to be a nurse to access the homes of her vulnerable victims.

3. Colombia's Medellin Cartel.

4. She turned them into bars of soap, giving them away to friends and neighbours, earning her the nickname 'The Soapmaker of Correggio'.

5. She lied about having cured her brain cancer with diet and natural remedies – but never had the disease. She was fined hundreds of thousands of pounds for making false claims.

6. Electroconvulsive therapy.

7. Samantha Lewthwaite.

8. The 7/7 terrorist attacks in London – she was married to suicide bomber Germaine Lindsay.

9. Linda Kasabian.

10. Dewsbury.

Quiz 19 – Women in Crime Whodunnit

Match these crime profiles to a perpetrator from the list below.

1. Eastender who started out as a getaway driver before turning her hand to armed robbery. She later shot her boyfriend Ronnie Cook in 1990 – a crime she has always denied – and was locked up for eighteen years for his murder. She was released in 2008 and is now going straight as a crime writer.

2. Went on a killing spree in Peterborough, murdering three men and dumping their bodies in ditches. She went on the run to Hereford where she tried to kill again – but her stabbing victims survived and she was apprehended by police. She was given a whole life order in February 2014, making her the first woman in British legal history to be given a whole life sentence directly in court.

3. Shot her boyfriend David Blakely to death in 1955 after meeting him through her hostess work in London nightclubs. The pair had a volatile relationship marred by domestic violence, which added to the sense of outrage when she was convicted of murder and sentenced to death. She was hanged at Holloway prison in July the same year.

4. Knifed a teenager to death in 1992 in an attack so savage police assumed a man had committed the crime. Later, while serving time for another stabbing, she bragged about having killed. Police found her diaries were packed with references to the 1992 murder. She was jailed for life with a fourteen-year tariff in 1997 and was branded 'The Devil's Daughter' by the media. She is considered Britain's youngest female murderer, aged only twelve when she killed.

5. Stabbed her boyfriend Lee Harvey to death and concocted a tale that they'd both been the victims of a road rage attack by a man with staring eyes. The police – and a jury – would have none of it and she was convicted of murder in July 1997. In 1999 she finally admitted the truth – she'd knifed Lee multiple times with a Swiss army knife.

6. Transgender champion fell runner who knifed UK athletics official Ralph Knibbs in the head and neck following a dispute over whether she could compete in women's races. She pleaded guilty to attempted murder and got eighteen years.

7. Conspired with her boyfriend Nathan Matthews to abduct his stepsister, Becky Watts. They killed the sixteen-year-old, and her dismembered body was found wrapped in clingfilm and hidden in suitcases. Matthews got life for murder. She was convicted of manslaughter and jailed for seventeen years.

8. Jailed in 2009 for causing or allowing the death of her own seventeen-month-old son, Peter – better known as 'Baby P', who died at their Tottenham home after months of abuse. She got an indefinite term of imprisonment for public protection. Boyfriend Steven Barker and his brother Jason Owen were also jailed for their part in Peter's death.

9. Walked into Labour MP Stephen Timms's constituency surgery in May 2010, smiled as she pretended she was going to shake hands with him and instead knifed him in the stomach. Timms thankfully made a recovery and even gave evidence at the trial, where his would-be killer was found guilty of attempted murder and jailed for life with a minimum of fifteen years.

10. Beat her lover Thomas Cressman with a cricket bat and stabbed him in the chest after he refused to marry her. She was jailed for murder in 2001 – a long fall from grace from her role as a royal aide to Sarah Ferguson, Duchess of York.

a) Ruth Ellis

b) Sharon Carr

c) Shauna Hoare

d) Jane Andrews

e) Lauren Jeska

f) Roshonara Choudhry

g) Joanna Dennehy

h) Tracie Andrews

i) Tracey Connelly

j) Linda Calvey

ANSWERS

1. j)

2. g)

3. a)

4. b)

5. h)

6. e)

7. c)

8. i)

9. f)

10. d)

HEISTS

There's something captivating about a big score caper – we can't fail to be intrigued by a well-planned heist and the rogues' gallery of shady characters in the crew behind it. Even after the spoils have been spent – and the crooks locked away – the sheer audacity of a genius take-down ensures it lives long in the memory.

Quiz 20 – Heists Trivia

1. Brian Reader is one of Britain's most prolific crooks and was jailed for his involvement in two of these famous heists – but he played no role in the other. Which is the odd one out?

   a) The Millennium Dome raid
   b) Hatton Garden
   c) Brink's-Mat

2. Which country did Ronald Biggs flee to after escaping Wandsworth Prison, a mere fifteen months into his thirty-year sentence for the Great Train Robbery?

   a) Brazil
   b) Belgium
   c) Australia

3. And what year did Biggs finally return to the UK to resume his jail sentence?

4. How many works of art – collectively worth $500-million – were stolen from Boston's Gardner Museum in 1990? For a bonus point, how many have been recovered?

5. Which Belgian city was the scene of the biggest diamond heist in world history, which took place in February 2003?

6. Where was John 'Goldfinger' Palmer extradited from to face trial accused of melting down stolen Brink's-Mat bullion?

   a) Tenerife
   b) Brazil
   c) Switzerland

7. Palmer was acquitted over his involvement in Brink's-Mat after admitting to smelting gold ingots but convincing the jury he didn't know they were stolen. He was, however, later jailed. What for?

8. The so-called Lufthansa Heist at New York's JFK airport in 1978 netted its suspected participants – linked to the Lucchese crime family – around $5.8 million in cash and jewels. The raid was a pivotal plot point in an all-time classic gangster movie. Which one?

9. What nationality were the trio behind the UK's biggest burglary spree, when a string of celebrity homes – including socialite Tamara Ecclestone's – were raided to the tune of twenty-six million pounds?

10. 'Diamond' Doris Payne travelled the world stealing gems from elite jewellers in a two-million-dollar criminal career spanning six decades. What was her first and only proper job?

    a) Miner
    b) Woolworths cashier
    c) Nurse

ANSWERS

1. a) Millennium Dome. In 1986 Reader got eight years for conspiracy to handle stolen gold bullion from Brink's-Mat and twenty-nine years later masterminded the fourteen-million-pound Hatton Garden safe deposit burglary – at the tender age of seventy-six!

2. b) Belgium. Biggs spent time in all three countries – eventually settling in Brazil – but Belgium was his first stop.

3. 2001.

4. Thirteen – and none have been recovered despite the museum's offer of a ten-million-dollar reward. Keep your eyes peeled!

5. Antwerp. Diamonds, gold and jewellery worth around a hundred million dollars were taken from the Antwerp Diamond Centre.

6. b) Brazil.

7. Timeshare fraud. In 2001 Palmer got eight years.

8. *Goodfellas*. Jimmy Burke – played by Robert De Niro – is thought to have masterminded the heist but was never charged.

9. Three Italian nationals were jailed in 2021 for the 2019 raid.

10. c) Nurse. Payne grew up in a mining town in West Virginia and worked in a nursing home in Cleveland.

Quiz 21 – Which Heist?

Pair each robbery description with an infamous big money job from the list below.

1. A team of five bank robbers spent three years planning their heist, studying the city's sewer network in a move said to be inspired by the Teenage Mutant Ninja Turtles. They struck in January 2006, taking a bunch of hostages. When police arrived on the scene, they convinced officers they were willing to surrender, but stalled for time by demanding food. When police busted in hours later they found the gang had vanished, escaping through the sewers with a reported twenty million dollars.

2. A gang posing as a landscape company rented a city centre property and spent three months tunnelling two blocks under the streets to a position below the bank. On the last weekend they busted through more than a metre of reinforced concrete to access the bank's vault and made off with cash equivalent to around seventy million dollars – but in local currency it weighed the equivalent of 3.5 tons!

3. Without a doubt the largest bank heist of all time – and possibly the least violent. But was it really a robbery? Experts are divided on that front; nonetheless, this is how it went down. A man arrived at the bank with a handwritten note from his father asking for a billion dollars in American dollars and euros. The sum represented a quarter of the country's entire cash reserves. Staff spent five hours loading the money onto three lorries which drove away with the loot.

4. Four gang members smashed into the premises on board a JCB digger, threw smoke bombs as a distraction and attempted to batter their way into a display case using a nail gun and sledgehammer. But unbeknown to the robbers, the gems inside were decoys, the police had been tipped off and armed officers were lying in wait. They quickly rounded up the thieves, including their getaway driver, who was waiting in a speedboat moored nearby.

5. Two men used a professional makeup artist to alter their appearance, claiming it was for a music video. Upon arriving at the scene of the robbery, they threatened staff with handguns and forced

them to open display cabinets to make off with rings, bracelets, watches and necklaces worth forty million pounds. Making their getaway, they fired shots into the air to create a distraction. They were caught after leaving a pay-as-you-go mobile phone – packed with tell-tale phone numbers – in one of their getaway cars.

6. One of the gang members managed to get a job working at their target organisation so he could pass on security info to his accomplices. A few months later, gang members posing as police officers abducted the manager and took him hostage, alongside his family. They used him to gain entry to the premises, tied up fourteen staff at gunpoint and filled a lorry with over fifty-three million pounds in used and unused notes. Police arrested a total of thirty-six suspects, leading to eight convictions – but less than half of the cash was recovered.

7. Another raid involving a hostage-taking. The families of two bank workers were held and the men were ordered to report for work as normal. As a test run, one filled a bag with a million pounds in notes and left it at a bus stop for the gang to pick up. The workers told colleagues to go home early and loaded trolleys with crates of bank notes. The gang drove a lorry into the loading bay and picked up the trolleys, returning later for a second run. In total, £26.5 million was taken and only two million pounds has been recovered. Only one man has ever been convicted in connection with the heist – for laundering stolen cash – and the robbers remain at large.

8. Two men walked into the premises and asked to rent a safety deposit box, but upon being shown the vault they pulled out handguns and overpowered security guards. They let in more accomplices and hung a 'closed' sign on the door, then smashed into safety deposit boxes to steal contents worth around sixty million pounds. Four men were later convicted. One, a prolific international robber, was caught when he brazenly returned to the UK to retrieve his prized Ferrari.

9. Two (or possibly three) security guards who slept at the premises overnight simply helped themselves to $282 million. No one has ever been convicted and against the background of a politically volatile moment in history, it's been suggested that government-level corruption was involved.

10. A feted bank robber got a tip from infamous, mobbed-up Teamster president Jimmy Hoffa that President Nixon had a thirty-million-dollar slush fund of dirty electoral campaign money stashed away. He put a team together, they tunnelled through the roof of the premises and spent the weekend relieving deposit boxes of around twelve million dollars. They were caught after they used similar methods to rob another bank just months later, and police linked the two.

a) Banco Central robbery, Fortaleza, Brazil.

b) Securitas depot robbery, Kent, 2006 – the UK's largest cash robbery.

c) Dar Es Salaam bank, Baghdad, 2007.

d) The Rio Banco heist in San Isidro, Buenos Aires.

e) The Knightsbridge Security Deposit robbery, London, 1987.

f) Central Bank of Iraq robbery, Baghdad, March 2003. The 'robber' was Qusay Hussein. His father – Saddam.

g) The Graff Diamonds Robbery, London, 2009.

h) Northern Bank Robbery, Belfast, 2004.

i) United California bank robbery, 1972.

j) The Millennium Dome raid, London, 2000.

ANSWERS

1. d)

2. a)

3. f)

4. j)

5. g)

6. b)

7. h)

8. e)

9. c)

10. i)

Quiz 22 – Art World Heists, Trivia Round

1. Which haunting Edvard Munch painting was stolen from an Oslo museum on the opening day of the 1994 Winter Olympics?

2. Which legendary neoclassical and surrealist painter was arrested over the 1911 theft of the *Mona Lisa* from the Louvre, but was ultimately exonerated?

3. In 1991, twenty paintings were stolen from a museum in the Netherlands, only to be recovered half an hour later in an abandoned getaway car. Which post-impressionist was the artist?

4. Which paramilitary group was behind the theft of nineteen artworks worth eight million pounds from the home of former Tory MP Sir Alfred Beit in 1974?

5. On Christmas Day in 1985, thieves crawled through air-conditioning ducts to make off with a priceless horde of 140 Mayan, Aztec, Miztec and Zapotec antiquities from a museum in which city?

   a) Lima
   b) Mexico City
   c) La Paz

6. What nickname did the French press give the athletically built Vjeran Tomic, who was jailed for eight years after admitting stealing artworks worth €104 million from the Musée d'Art Moderne in Paris in 2010?

7. Where were three artworks stolen from Manchester's Whitworth Art Gallery in 2003 – including a Van Gogh watercolour worth two million pounds – found just hours later?

   a) In a soggy cardboard tube in a public toilet
   b) In an old record box in the defunct Hacienda nightclub
   c) Under a bush in Piccadilly Gardens

8. Which museum in Dresden, Germany was the scene of an audacious art jewellery theft in 2019 in which gems and royal regalia worth a reported €113 million were stolen?

9. What do police believe happened to the three-million-pound Henry Moore sculpture, *Reclining Figure*, which was stolen from Much Hadham, Hertfordshire, in 2005?

10. Name the Van Gogh painting pinched from Cairo's Mohamed Mahmoud Khalil Museum in 1977 and recovered a decade later in Kuwait, only to be stolen again in 2010.

ANSWERS

1. *The Scream*. The thieves left a note which read, 'Thousand thanks for the bad security.' The painting was recovered a few months later.

2. Pablo Picasso. Suspicion fell on him thanks to his purchases of other paintings from an artist with a history of stealing from the gallery. Italian handyman Vincenzo Peruggia – who worked at the Louvre – was later unmasked as the real thief.

3. Vincent van Gogh.

4. The IRA.

5. b) Mexico City.

6. Spider-Man.

7. a) They were in the loo just two hundred metres away, along with a note from the thieves saying they merely wanted to highlight the lax security.

8. Green Vault Museum.

9. Inquiries suggested the statue was sold through scrapyards and melted down – perhaps for as little as £1,500.

10. *Poppy Flowers*. It's worth fifty-five million dollars and it's still missing.

Quiz 23 – The Great Train Robbery

1. What board game did the train robbers play as they hid out in the aftermath of the heist, reportedly using the spoils of their crime in place of toy banknotes?

2. Which table condiment is said to have given the crooks away by revealing a number of tell-tale fingerprints to investigating cops?

3. What is the name of the farm where the gang split up their cash?

   a) Willingdon Farm
   b) Leatherslade Farm
   c) Grange Spinney Farm

4. What year did the robbery take place?

   a) 1963
   b) 1966
   c) 1969

5. Roughly how much would the £2.6 million stolen be worth in today's money?

6. How many shots were fired by the gang in committing the robbery?

7. What injury did train driver Jack Mills suffer at the hands of one of the robbers?

8. The train was heading from London to Glasgow on the west coast main line when it was robbed. Which English county did the robbers stop the train in?

9. Which train robber's son would grow up to join the band Alabama 3, which ironically provided the theme tune for seminal mob drama *The Sopranos*?

10. In later life, and having served nine years of a fifteen-year sentence, outside which London railway station would you have found Ronald 'Buster' Edwards running his flower stall?

ANSWERS

1. Monopoly.

2. A bottle of ketchup.

3. b) Leatherslade Farm.

4. a) 1963.

5. Approximately forty-four million pounds, according to the Bank of England.

6. None. They didn't carry guns.

7. He was beaten across the head with a metal bar after putting up a fight. He never fully returned to work and died seven years later from leukaemia.

8. Buckinghamshire.

9. Bruce Reynolds's son, Nick.

10. Waterloo.

Quiz 24 – Brink's-Mat

1. What is the name of the trading estate where the Brink's-Mat bullion heist took place? Clue – it shares its name with an international airport.

2. How much did the 6,840 gold ingots stolen by the gang weigh?

   a) 1 tonne   b) 2 tonnes   c) 3 tonnes

3. In which south-west city in England did 'Goldfinger' John Palmer have his jewellery business, Scadlynn, used as a front to launder the spoils of the robbery?

4. What names did Brink's-Mat robber Jimmy McAvoy reportedly give to his two rottweiler guard dogs in the wake of the robbery?

5. What fate befell Detective Constable John Fordham during a surveillance operation on the home of gangster Kenneth Noye, who police suspected was handling the stolen bullion?

6. Noye was eventually jailed for fourteen years for conspiracy to handle stolen gold but two years after his release went on the run after committing another heinous crime. What?

7. What was the value of the gold stolen by the gang?

   a) £11 million   b) £18 million   c) £26 million

8. What did the gang do to strike fear into one of the security officers guarding the depot and convince him to open the safe?

9. What was the name of the 'inside man', a security guard who worked in the depot and allowed the gang to gain entry?

   a) Tony White   b) Tony Black   c) Tony Greene

10. It took police a week to work out that John Palmer – gunned down in the garden of his home – had been murdered, despite six bullet holes riddling his body. What did they supposedly 'mistake' the wounds for, concluding he died of natural causes?

    a) Scars from gallbladder surgery
    b) Tomato ketchup
    c) A nosebleed

ANSWERS

1. Heathrow International Trading Estate.

2. c)   3 tonnes.

3. Bristol.

4. Brinks and Mat.

5. Noye stabbed him to death, knifing the officer eleven times. He was cleared of murder after claiming self-defence.

6. He stabbed motorist Stephen Cameron to death in a road rage incident. He was brought to justice four years later after police tracked him to his Spanish hideaway and was jailed for life in 2000.

7. c)   £26 million, or £84 million in today's money!

8. Doused him in petrol.

9. b)   Tony Black.

10. a)   Scars from gallbladder surgery.

PARTNERS IN CRIME

Two's company for these criminal couples and double acts...

Quiz 25 – Partners in Crime, Trivia

1. How were multiple murderers Richard 'Dick' Hickock and Perry Smith executed after being convicted of slaughtering the Clutter family, a crime later immortalised by Truman Capote in his book, *In Cold Blood*?

2. Elderly Faye and Ray Copeland of Missouri became America's oldest serial killers when they were convicted, aged sixty-nine and seventy-six, in 1990 and 1991 of murdering five farmhand drifters – but what did Faye do with the victims after Ray shot them in the head with his .22 calibre rifle?

    a) Turned them into stew
    b) Fed them to their pigs
    c) Made a quilt from their clothes

3. Police initially thought just one serial killer was acting alone in terrorising LA between 1977–78, with the media dubbing the fiend the 'Hillside Strangler'. However, two men were eventually brought to justice for kidnapping, torturing and murdering ten women – how were they related?

4. Which infamous high school shooting massacre are Eric Harris and Dylan Klebold known for?

5. What nickname was given to multiple rapists, serial killers and lifelong friends John Duffy and David Mulcahy, who attacked numerous women in southern England in the eighties?

6. Twelve-year-old Jasmine Richardson reportedly became Canada's youngest multiple murderer in 2006 after slaughtering her parents and brother in cahoots with her twenty-three-year-old boyfriend, Jeremy Steinke. What mythical man-beast did Steinke style himself on?

7. Australia's own house of horrors is in Moorhouse Street, Perth, where in 1986 a husband and wife double act murdered four women. The alarm was raised when their fifth would-be victim escaped. What were the couple called?

8. How did killer couple Bailey Boswell and her swinger boyfriend Aubrey Trail meet their victim, Sydney Loofe?

9. How are ex-couple Karla Homolka and Paul Bernardo – involved in the rape and killing of at least two girls in Canada, including Karla's sister, Tammy – better known?

10. How did 'Toy Box Killer' David Parker Ray – who committed his crimes with his girlfriend, Cindy Hendy, acting as an accomplice – earn his nickname?

ANSWERS

1. They were hanged at Leavenworth prison in Kansas after five years on death row.

2. c) Made a quilt from their clothes. The pair both got death sentences, but Ray died of natural causes. Faye's sentence was commuted to life following an appeal. She died in a nursing home after suffering a stroke.

3. Kenneth Bianchi and Angelo Buono Jr. were cousins.

4. Columbine.

5. The Railway Rapists. They often attacked near railway stations.

6. He reportedly claimed to be a three-hundred-year-old werewolf and wore a vial of blood around his neck. (Other accounts have him as a vampire – score a point for either.)

7. David and Catherine Birnie.

8. She was lured by Boswell on Tinder before being murdered and dismembered.

9. The 'Barbie Killers'. Bernardo – separately known as the 'Scarborough Rapist' – was jailed for life. Karla took a plea deal and got twelve years for manslaughter, claiming she had been an unwilling accomplice. They were never arrested or charged over Tammy's death, which was deemed an accident, but Karla's twelve-year sentence reportedly took Tammy's death into account.

10. He had a shipping container where he abused and tortured his victims. Ray got over two hundred years' prison for kidnap and torture, but never admitted murder. He died shortly after he was sentenced. Hendy got thirty-six years for criminal sexual penetration and kidnapping.

Quiz 26 – Match the Pairs

Pair up these criminal couples and double acts. To make things a little tougher, we've given you just their first or last names only.

1. Robert

2. Ian

3. Parker

4. Fernandez

5. Starkweather

6. Susan

7. Jesse

8. Butch

9. Clark

10. Maxine

a) Beck

b) Christopher

c) Fugate

d) Barrow

e) Harry

f) Bundy

g) Jon

h) Ian

i) Frank

j) Myra

ANSWERS

1. g) Robert Thompson and Jon Venables – the child killers murdered toddler Jamie Bulger.

2. j) Ian Brady and Myra Hindley – the Moors murderers themselves.

3. d) Bonnie Parker and Clyde Barrow – better known as Bonnie and Clyde.

4. a) Raymond Fernandez and Martha Beck – the so-called 'Lonely Hearts Killers' met their victims through personal ads in the US in the late 1940s.

5. c) Charles Starkweather and Caril Ann Fugate – this ill-fated couple went on a killing spree across Nebraska and Wyoming in 1958.

6. b) Susan Edwards and Christopher Edwards – both serving life for murdering Susan's parents.

7. i) Jesse James and Frank James – gunslinging brothers who became infamous Wild West outlaws.

8. e) Butch Cassidy and Harry Alonzo Longabaugh – another gunslinging, Wild West double act, Longabaugh is of course better known as the 'Sundance Kid'.

9. f) Douglas Clark and Carol Bundy – dubbed the 'Sunset Strip Killers', this pair killed a string of LA sex workers and prostitutes in 1980.

10. h) Maxine Carr and Ian Huntley – Huntley killed schoolgirls Holly Wells and Jessica Chapman in Soham, Cambridgeshire. Maxine Carr was jailed for perverting the course of justice after giving Huntley a false alibi.

ASSASSINATIONS

The loss of a hero or leader burns bright in the public consciousness, its impact often sending shockwaves around the world, so it's little wonder that we reserve a special term for these acts of murder: assassinations.

Quiz 27 – Assassinations Trivia

1. Archduke Franz Ferdinand and his wife were famously shot dead by Slavic nationalist Gavrilo Princip in June 1914, triggering World War I. However, the pair had survived an earlier assassination bid just hours before – what method had the would-be killer used?

2. What art form links the circumstances of Abraham Lincoln's assassination with his killer, John Wilkes Booth?

3. Four years before Lee Harvey Oswald shot President John F. Kennedy, he tried his hand at living overseas. Where?

   a) North Korea
   b) Cuba
   c) USSR

4. How many assassination attempts did Mahatma Gandhi survive before he was shot dead by Nathuram Godse in January 1948?

5. What nationality is Mehmet Ali Ağca, the would-be assassin who tried – and failed – to assassinate Pope John Paul II in 1981?

6. In what city was killer James Earl Ray finally arrested two months after shooting dead civil rights leader Martin Luther King in Memphis in 1968?

7. Which fictional literary misfit did John Lennon's killer Mark David Chapman model himself on?

   a) Holden Caulfield, from *The Catcher in the Rye*
   b) Tom Ripley, from *The Talented Mr Ripley*
   c) Joe Buck, from *Midnight Cowboy*

8. Who was the intended target of would-be assassin Samuel Byck? In 1974 he tried to hijack a plane with the aim of crashing it, kamikaze-style, in a plot eerily reminiscent of 9/11.

9. What was the cartoon character nickname of Pablo Escobar's top hitman, Jhon Jairo Velásquez, who confessed to the murders of nearly 260 victims, including the assassination of presidential candidate Luis Carlos Galán?

10. Name the beloved British royal killed alongside three members of his holiday party in 1979 when their boat was blown up with fifty pounds of gelignite planted by the IRA.

ANSWERS

1. Princip's brother-in-arms Nedjelko Čabrinović lobbed a grenade at the Archduke's car, but it bounced off and exploded under the following vehicle.

2. Theatre. Booth was an acclaimed actor. He shot the American president in the head as he took his seat for an evening performance at Ford's Theatre, Washington DC.

3. c) USSR. Oswald defected and married in Minsk, but returned to the US in 1962 with his wife and their daughter.

4. Five. Gandhi dodged bombs, attempted stabbings and an attempted train derailment. Two of the earlier assassination bids were committed by his eventual killer.

5. Turkish.

6. London (at Heathrow Airport). He fled Canada after the killing and then hid out in Lisbon and London.

7. a) Holden Caulfield. Police found Chapman at the scene of the killing apparently reading a copy of Salinger's landmark novel.

8. President Nixon. Byck planned to crash the plane into the White House. His bid failed but he shot and killed a security officer and a pilot in the process, before taking his own life.

9. 'Popeye'. Velásquez died of cancer in 2020. Besides his personal death toll, he claimed to have been involved in planning over three thousand killings.

10. Lord Louis Mountbatten.

Quiz 28 – Match The Victim to The Method

Pair these victims of assassination with the instrument used by their killer from the list below.

1. Julius Caesar

2. Leon Trotsky

3. Alexander Litvinenko

4. Kim Jong-nam

5. Giovanni Falcone

6. Georgi Markov

7. Jörg Jenatsch

8. Thomas of Woodstock, Duke of Gloucester

9. Daphne Caruana Galizia

10. Grigori Rasputin

a) Nerve agent

b) Car bomb

c) Dagger

d) Ricin

e) Cyanide, shooting and drowning

f) Bear with an axe

g) Polonium-210

h) TNT and Semtex

i) Mattress

j) Ice axe

ANSWERS

1. c) Julius Caesar was knifed to death by a group of Roman senators.

2. j) An ice axe blow to the head finished off Marxist revolutionary Trotsky.

3. g) The Russian dissident suffered a slow and agonising death after being poisoned with the radioactive isotope.

4. a) Kim Jong-nam, the eldest son of North Korean leader Kim Jong II, was smeared with the nerve agent VX.

5. h) The Sicilian mafia took out the judge, his wife and their police escort by blowing up a motorway.

6. d) Markov – a Bulgarian dissident and writer – was stabbed in the leg with a poison-tipped umbrella in a plot straight out of a James Bond movie.

7. f) The seventeenth-century Swiss politician's assailant was actually a man in a bear suit.

8. i) The Duke was smothered under a feather bed in 1397, most likely at the behest of King Richard II.

9. b) A bomb planted under her car seat killed Malta's foremost investigative journalist and anti-corruption activist in 2017.

10. e) The Russian mystic was shot when cyanide failed to kill him, but finally died by drowning when he was tied up and thrown in a river.

DRUGS

The global trade in illegal drugs stacks up to a whopping $650 billion a year – any wonder that it makes such a tempting proposition for the criminally-inclined?

Quiz 29 – Drug Lords

Match these five drug lords, smugglers and dealers to the substance they're best known for from the list below.

1. Charles Forsman

2. Haji Bagcho

3. Alston Hughes

4. Tom Forcade

5. Lori Arnold

a) Heroin

b) Cannabis

c) Methamphetamine

d) Cocaine

e) LSD

Now match these five kingpins to their nationality . . .

6. Augusto Falcon

7. Howard Marks

8. Dawood Ibrahim

9. Khun Sa

10. Amado Carrillo Fuentes

f) Indian

g) Cuban

h) Mexican

i) Welsh

j) Burmese

ANSWERS

1. d) Forsman's coke-smuggling exploits were chronicled in the book *Snowblind* where he was given the pseudonym Zachary Swan.

2. a) At one time, Afghan Bagcho was said to be behind 20 per cent of the world's heroin supply.

3. e) Alston Hughes AKA 'Smiles' was a leading light in a 1970s' LSD ring.

4. b) Forcade not only smuggled weed but founded a magazine about it – the counter-culture legend *High Times.*

5. c) At one point the the 'Queen of Meth' made $200,000 a week peddling the drug in America's midwest.

6. g) Cuban Falcon ran a massive coke smuggling operation in Miami in the mid-eighties.

7. i) Marks was born in Kenfig Hill, South Wales.

8. f) Ibrahim is said to have founded Mumbai crime syndicate, D-Company.

9. j) The Golden Triangle warlord controlled 70 per cent of the world's heroin supply for two decades.

10. h) Fuentes' skill at smuggling cocaine from Colombia made him a multi-billionaire.

Quiz 30 – Drugs Trivia

1. Name the British kingpin who amassed such vast wealth he became the only drug trafficker in history to make it on to the *Sunday Times* 'Rich List'.

2. In 1977 police dismantled a drugs ring in rural west Wales, seizing enough crystal LSD to make 6.5 million tabs – the biggest acid bust the world had ever seen at the time. What was the name of the police operation?

3. What name have psychonauts the world over given to 19 April, in honour of Swiss chemist Albert Hoffman, who took the first ever intentional LSD trip on that day in 1938?

4. What was the name of the former Trans World Airlines pilot who smuggled cocaine for Pablo Escobar before meeting a sticky end at the behest of the Medellin Cartel in 1986?

   a) George Jung
   b) Gary Betzner
   c) Barry Seal

5. Lands around Pablo Escobar's vast estate are being overrun by which native African creature after the flamboyant drug lord introduced a handful of them in the 1980s?

6. What was the name of the Metropolitan police drug squad officer who famously busted some of the swinging sixties' biggest celebrities – including John Lennon and Brian Jones – before falling from grace and being jailed for perjury?

   a) Norman Pilcher
   b) Brian Plant
   c) Thomas Butler

7. Rolling Stone Keith Richards was busted for drugs at his Sussex country pile alongside bandmate Mick Jagger in 1967. What was the property called?

    a) Badlands
    b) Henlands
    c) Redlands

8. What was the title of legendary cannabis smuggler Howard Marks's biography?

9. In which notoriously tough American prison did Marks serve seven years of a twenty-five-year sentence?

    a) Riker
    b) Terre Haute
    c) Alcatraz

10. Drug lord Joaquín 'El Chapo' Guzmán headed up which Mexican cartel until his arrest and incarceration?

ANSWERS

1. Curtis Warren was listed in 1997 as a 'property developer' with a forty-million-pound fortune.

2. Operation Julie.

3. 'Bicycle Day' – Hoffman rode home from his lab experiencing 'kaleidoscopic, fantastic images'.

4. c) Barry Seal.

5. Hippopotamuses.

6. a) Norman 'Nobby' Pilcher.

7. c) Redlands.

8. *Mr Nice.*

9. b) Terre Haute.

10. The Sinaloa Cartel.

Quiz 31 – Drugs Trivia, Round Two

1. What year was medical cannabis legalised in the UK?

2. Name the infamous darknet drug marketplace masterminded by Ross Ulbricht until it was busted by the FBI in 2013.

3. What username did Ulbricht use to communicate with users of the site?

4. In 1978, after being jailed for thirteen years for making millions of doses of LSD, this British chemist released a statement foretelling many of today's environmental problems and suggesting the psychedelic drug was a catalyst for change. His name was . . .

   a) Francis Crick
   b) Timothy Leary
   c) Richard Kemp

5. Name the American author who famously held LSD-laced parties in mid-sixties' San Francisco and Los Angeles which he called 'Acid Tests'.

   a) Ken Kesey
   b) Tom Wolfe
   c) Aldous Huxley

6. Pablo Escobar headed up Colombia's Medellin cartel. Who were his bitter rivals, the two brothers who led the Cali cartel, and who were ultimately extradited to the US to serve thirty-year prison sentences?

7. What was the name given to the Marseille-based global drug network run by Corsican gangsters which dominated the supply of heroin to the US from the late 1940s through to the 1970s?

8. What was the anti-drugs advertising campaign which became famous during the Reagan era in the US and even led to a top-five chart hit in the UK for the cast of BBC school drama *Grange Hill* with a song of the same name?

9. What nickname did drug lord Amado Carrillo Fuentes earn thanks to his fleet of Boeing 727 airliners, used to traffic cocaine?

10. Which family of American billionaires agreed to pay six billion dollars to resolve civil litigation alleging that they fuelled the US opioid epidemic through deceptive marketing of their company's pain medicine, Oxycontin?

ANSWERS

1. 2018.

2. Silk Road.

3. Dread Pirate Roberts.

4. c) Richard Kemp. His eight-thousand-word mitigation was précised in local paper the *Cambrian News*.

5. a) Ken Kesey held the parties. Tom Wolfe wrote about them in *The Electric Kool-Aid Acid Test*.

6. Gilberto and Miguel Orejuela.

7. The French Connection.

8. 'Just Say No' – the campaign was launched and popularised by First Lady Nancy Reagan.

9. *'El Señor de Los Cielos'* ('Lord of the Skies').

10. The Sacklers. They deny any personal wrongdoing. Their company, Purdue, pleaded guilty to criminal charges concerning its marketing of the drug.

WHITE COLLAR CRIME

Some crooks just don't like getting their hands dirty – some are more than happy to take your cash wearing a suit and a smile.

Quiz 32 – White Collar Crime Trivia

1. Which sixty-billion-dollar American energy giant collapsed in 2001 after using shady accounting to hide piles of debt and toxic assets from its hapless investors?

2. What was the full name of the Italian businessman whose surname became synonymous with a well-known financial scam promising massive returns; in reality early investors are paid with cash taken from later investors?

3. Which American financier masterminded the largest scam of the type in the previous question – valued at almost sixty-five billion dollars – earning him a whopping 150-year jail sentence?

4. Name the international bank with HQs in London and Karachi which spectacularly imploded in 1991 amid regulatory investigations which exposed its involvement in money laundering for everyone from druglords to dictators.

5. Which UK-based high-street bank agreed in 2012 to pay a controversial $1.9-billion fine to settle allegations it enabled the laundering of millions of dollars for the Sinaloa drugs cartel and other Mexican kingpins?

6. Name the British stock market trader jailed for six-and-a-half years after his increasingly risky trades cost Barings Bank $1.4 billion, causing its collapse.

7. How did conman Edward Putman cheat the UK's National Lottery out of £2.5 million in 2009, a crime which later earned him nine years in prison?

8. Who was the American home decor guru jailed for five months in 2004 for felony charges relating to an insider trading scandal?

9. What was the supposed purpose of the failed medical gizmo devised by Theranos founder Elizabeth Holmes, convicted of defrauding investors out of hundreds of millions of dollars?

10. Name the Bulgarian-based fraudulent cryptocurrency which operated as a massive pyramid scheme to con victims all over the world out of four billion dollars.

ANSWERS

1. Enron. Various execs were indicted, with some receiving prison sentences.

2. Charles Ponzi (AKA Carlo Ponzi and Charles Ponci).

3. Bernie Madoff. He died in prison in 2021.

4. BCCI – the Bank of Credit and Commerce International.

5. HSBC. No HSBC banker has ever been prosecuted over the scandal.

6. Nick Leeson.

7. He cashed in a fake ticket with the help of lottery insider Giles Knibbs, who later took his own life after confessing to pals.

8. Martha Stewart. She denied insider trading and the judge dismissed that charge, but she was found guilty of conspiracy, obstruction of justice and two counts of making false statements.

9. It was for testing blood.

10. OneCoin. Co-founder Karl Greenwood admitted wire fraud and money laundering in December 2022. His alleged partner in crime, Ruja Ignatova has been missing since 2017 and is on the FBI's list of ten most wanted fugitives – with a $100,000 reward on her head.

ACTS OF TERROR

Violence has been used for centuries to send a message or achieve a political goal. It's part of the toolbox of revolutionaries, radicals and deranged lone wolves.

Quiz 33 – Terror Trivia

1. Beginning his terror campaign in the late 1970s, Ted Kaczysnki targeted American universities and airlines with homemade bombs. The FBI finally caught up with him in 1996. By what nickname was he better known?

2. Which country were the far-left guerilla group Red Army Faction – also known as the Baader-Meinhof gang – active in? They were around in the 1970s and 1980s before calling an end to their campaign of bombings, abductions and assassinations in 1992.

3. WPC Yvonne Fletcher was policing a demonstration outside which central London foreign embassy when she was shot dead in April 1984?

4. In March 1995, followers of the Japanese doomsday cult Aum Shinrikyo launched a coordinated attack on the Tokyo subway which killed thirteen. What weapon did they use?

5. Which American pop singer performed at the Manchester Arena before suicide bomber Salman Abedi detonated a device in the foyer, killing twenty-two, in May 2017?

6. Name the seaside town targeted in another bomb attack, this time by the IRA, in October 1984.

7. Far right extremist and domestic terrorist Anders Breivik killed seventy-seven in a gun and bomb rampage in 2011 – in which country?

8. Name the Palestinian militant group behind the 1972 Munich Olympics massacre when eleven Israeli athletes and coaches were shot dead.

9. Months after the 9/11 attacks, Briton Richard Reid attempted to blow up American Airlines flight 63 with improvised explosive devices. Where were they concealed?

10. What name did the media give to Venezuelan-born Marxist militant Ilich Ramírez Sánchez, active in Europe for twelve years from 1973 and famous for taking sixty hostages in a raid on OPEC's Vienna HQ in 1975?

ANSWERS

1. The Unabomber, from the task force assigned to the case – UNABOM.

2. West Germany.

3. Libyan.

4. Sarin nerve gas.

5. Ariana Grande.

6. Brighton: they bombed the Grand Hotel, hosting that year's Conservative Party conference.

7. Norway.

8. Black September.

9. In his shoes.

10. Carlos the Jackal.

Quiz 34 – Terror Trivia, UK Edition

1. What was the codename given to the SAS operation which brought the Iranian embassy siege of 1980 to a dramatic conclusion?

    a) Operation Narcissus
    b) Operation Telic
    c) Operation Nimrod

2. For a point apiece, name the two Birmingham pubs targeted by the IRA in two separate bomb attacks on 21 November 1974, killing twenty-one.

3. What flight number was the Pan Am plane blown up over Lockerbie, Scotland, in December 1988?

4. The first suicide attacks on British soil were carried out where and in what year?

5. Which north-west town was rocked by two successive bombings in consecutive months in early 1993?

6. Which British prime minister was the target of an Islamist suicide plot foiled by secret services?

7. In 1996, which British city became the scene of the biggest mainland bomb since World War II?

8. In what year did London nail bomber David Copeland bring terror to the capital's LGBT, black and Asian communities over three successive April weekends?

9. Which anti-fascist pressure group helped foil a neo-nazi terror plot to murder MP Rosie Cooper?

10. Name the leading light of the literary scene who was the intended target of an explosion which took out two floors of a London hotel in 1989, killing the bomber.

ANSWERS

1. c)   Operation Nimrod.

2. The Mulberry Bush and the Tavern in the Town.

3. Flight 103.

4. London, 2005 – the 7/7 bombings which killed fifty-two.

5. Warrington.

6. Theresa May, in 2017.

7. Manchester, carried out by the IRA.

8. 1999.

9. Hope Not Hate.

10. Salman Rushdie.

ORGANISED CRIME

Crime as big business. Crime incorporated. For a select few major underworld players operating at the highest echelons, crime really does pay. Getting there takes cunning, intelligence and – inevitably – the willingness to spill a little blood along the way.

Quiz 35 – Organised Crime Trivia

1. Which Italian city is the stronghold of the Camorra organised crime group?

2. Name the crusading Italian journalist who has a price on his head after his book, *Gomorrah*, exposed the Camorra's inner workings.

3. Who was the ironically named Jamaican drug lord extradited to the US in 2010 following a battle between his private army and the Jamaican military which left seventy-three civilians dead?

4. How did Swedish hitman Anis Hemissi disguise himself to reconnoitre his assassination of organised crime rival Flamur Beqiri in Battersea, London, on Christmas Eve 2019?

   a) As a pizza delivery man
   b) As a double-glazing salesman
   c) As a litter picker

5. What was the unlikely black market commodity behind the 1995 organised crime murder of Belgian meat inspector Karel Van Noppen?

6. From which South American country was so-called 'cocaine king of Milan' Rocco Morabito extradited from in 2022?

7. What global sporting event was Russian businessman and suspected crime kingpin Alimzhan Tokhtakhunov – currently subject of a four-million-dollar reward offer from the US State Department over alleged links to money laundering – accused of fixing?

   a) The Winter Olympics
   b) The World Cup
   c) The Grand Prix

8. What special skill did feted nineties' Russian hitman Alexander 'Sasha the Macedonian' Solonik possess that undoubtedly helped him achieve his 'Superkiller' title?

9. What was the name of the secret encrypted phone network favoured by organised criminals until it was compromised by law enforcement in 2020, leading to thousands of arrests across Europe and almost three thousand in the UK alone?

10. The year 2022 marked the first instances of so-called 'FGC-9' 3D-printed submachine guns appearing on UK streets. But what does the acronym 'FGC-9' stand for?

ANSWERS

1. Naples.

2. Roberto Saviano. The book inspired a five-season TV series of the same name.

3. Christopher 'Dudus' Coke, currently serving twenty-three years in a federal US prison for trafficking cocaine and marijuana.

4. c) Litter picker. Now serving life, with a minimum of thirty-five years, for murder.

5. Growth hormones. The EU outlawed the use of several hormones in cattle production, leading to a lucrative – and deadly – black market.

6. Brazil.

7. a) He was arrested in Italy in 2002 on suspicion of conspiring to fix the pairs figure-skating contest at the Winter Olympics in Salt Lake City. US prosecutors requested his extradition but he was released by Italian authorities and is thought to be at large in Russia.

8. He could shoot with both hands and used a pistol in each.

9. EncroChat.

10. Fuck Gun Control 9-mm.

Quiz 36 – North of Watford, Trivia

Tales abound of London blaggers, but this trivia round takes you beyond the capital to the gangs of the Midlands, the north and Scotland.

1. Contract killer Mark 'Iceman' Fellows got a whole life term in 2019 for the murders of Salford's Paul Massey and John Kinsella from Liverpool. His downfall came, in part, thanks to evidence police found on which electronic gizmo?

2. In his heyday, Paul Massey and his 'Salford firm' were said to be the power behind the muscle controlling the doors of which legendary northern rave venue?

3. That muscle was provided by three brothers, whose first names all begin with D. What's the surname?

4. Name the Manchester suburb that is home to the Gooch Close Gang who rose to infamy in the 1990s, their career culminating in 2009 murder convictions for lynchpins Colin Joyce and Lee Amos.

5. Which feared Glasgow-based gangster survived a 1966 attempt on his life by car-bombing which killed his mother-in-law?

6. Two Glasgow families are said to be behind Scotland's most notorious organised crime gangs. The two families are:

    a) Lyons and Daniel
    b) Campbell and Murray
    c) Walker and McVitie

7. Which English city is home to the Burger Bar Boys and rival Johnson Crew?

8. Teenagers Charlene Ellis and Letisha Shakespeare were innocent bystanders gunned down in a drive-by shooting which was part of a feud between these two warring rivals. What year were they killed?

    a) 2001
    b) 2005
    c) 2003

9. What Scottish city would you head to for a rumble with street gangs Clerry Jungle and Young Niddrie Terror?

10. What is the name of the National Crime Agency 'most wanted' fugitive who links the Liverpool murders of Liam Kelly in 2004 and Lucy Hargreaves in 2005?

    a) Christian Parnell
    b) Kevin Parle
    c) Colin Poole

ANSWERS

1. His Garmin fitness watch, which recorded him carrying out reconnaissance on Massey's home.

2. The Haçienda.

3. Noonan. Damien and Dessie died in 2004 and 2005 respectively. Dominic got eleven years in 2015 for arson, blackmail and perverting the course of justice. He was given another eleven years in 2018 for historic sex offences against young boys.

4. Moss Side.

5. Arthur Thompson.

6. a) Lyons and Daniel.

7. Birmingham.

8. c) 2003.

9. Edinburgh.

10. b) Kevin Parle. He is wanted for both murders.

Quiz 37 – American Gangster

1. The 'Al' in Al Capone is short for . . .

   a) Alfredo
   b) Alessio
   c) Alphonse

2. He survived shootings, stabbings and various assassination attempts, but what lethal infectious disease hastened Al Capone's demise in his late forties, leaving him with the mental capacity of a twelve-year-old?

3. What name has been given to the blood-soaked episode in February 1929 when seven members of Chicago's North Side gang were lined up against a wall and executed by four gunmen dressed as cops?

4. How was the elite squad of US Bureau of Prohibition agents headed up by Eliot Ness and tasked with taking down Al Capone better known?

5. Name the legendary, mob-owned Greenwich Village bar which in 1969 became the centre of a riotous uprising and the birthplace of the modern LGBTQ+ rights movement.

6. How did the so-called 'Odd Father' Vincent Gigante – boss of the Genovese crime family and one of the most successful mob dons in US history – earn his unusual nickname?

   a) He had three nipples
   b) He pretended to be mad
   c) He always bet odd numbers at roulette

7. What nefarious CIA mind-control programme did feared Boston mobster James 'Whitey' Bulger claim to have taken part in in exchange for a reduced sentence?

8. What ruse did Great Depression-era gangster and bank robber John Dillinger use to escape prison?

    a) Swapped clothes with his mother during a prison visit
    b) Carved a fake gun from a piece of scrap wood
    c) Climbed in a coffin with a dead body in the prison mortuary

9. Which white supremacist organisation did Colombo family mobster Gregory Scarpa reportedly shake down at the behest of the FBI to help locate the missing bodies of three slain civil rights workers in Mississippi in 1964?

10. Which legendary jazz hornsman got an early career break at New Orleans saloon, Matranga's, owned by Sicilian mobster Henry Matranga?

ANSWERS

1. c) Alphonse.

2. He died aged forty-eight of cardiac arrest, but not before syphilis destroyed his brain.

3. Saint Valentine's Day Massacre.

4. The Untouchables.

5. The Stonewall Inn. Gay bars were largely illegal in the sixties. Mobsters saw an opportunity and opened several, including the Stonewall, which was controlled by New York's Genovese family.

6. b) He feigned insanity to throw cops off the scent and was often seen wandering New York in a dressing gown and slippers, muttering to himself, as part of the act.

7. MK-Ultra. He claimed to have been injected with multiple doses of LSD as part of the experiments.

8. b) He carved a gun and used it to trick his guards, relieving them of their machine guns.

9. The Ku Klux Klan.

10. Louis Armstrong.

Quiz 38 – Match the Nations

Which country do you associate these organised crime groups with? Pair them to the list below.

1. Solntsevskaya Bratva

2. Yakuza

3. Los Zetas

4. 'Ndrangheta

5. Abergil Organisation

6. Red Command

7. Clan del Golfo

8. Black Axe

9. Penose

10. Los Charlines

a) Japan

b) Nigeria

c) Israel

d) Russia

e) Netherlands

f) Colombia

g) Spain

h) Italy

i) Mexico

j) Brazil

ANSWERS

1. d)

2. a)

3. i)

4. h)

5. c)

6. j)

7. f)

8. b)

9. e)

10. g)

Quiz 39 – Gangs of London, Trivia

1. In March 1966, Ronnie Kray walked into an East End pub and shot rival George Cornell in the forehead with a 9-mm Luger. What is the name of the pub where Cornell had his fateful last pint?

   a) The Carpenter's Arms
   b) The Ten Bells
   c) The Blind Beggar

2. Ronnie was brought to justice in March 1969 and jailed for life alongside his brother, Reggie. However, Reggie was convicted of an entirely different murder. Whose?

   a) Jack McVitie
   b) Freddie Foreman
   c) 'Mad' Frankie Fraser

3. What was the family name of the Kray Twins' principal rivals, headed up by brothers Charlie and Eddie?

4. Before the Krays rose to power, Jack Comer, AKA Jacob Colmore – arguably the architect of modern organised crime in the UK – ruled the roost. He was born to Jewish immigrants in London in 1912. Which country had his parents fled to escape anti-Jewish pogroms?

5. Name the ex-enforcer and armed robber who led the Chaps in 1970s' north London, but became an anti-crime campaigner after prison and penned a 2014 autobiography, *I Am Not a Gangster*.

6. An all-female syndicate of ace shoplifters who raided the West End's exclusive stores enjoyed their heyday in the interwar period. They were known as the Forty . . . what?

   a) Dippers
   b) Footpads
   c) Elephants

7. What British gangster film did notorious East End hard man and bare-knuckle boxer Lenny McLean star in as enforcer Barry the Baptist – only to die of lung cancer shortly before the film's 1998 release?

8. McLean's talents weren't limited to acting and street brawling: he also recorded an album of covers by a legendary, hip-swinging rock'n'roller. Who?

9. So-called 'Jigsaw Man' murderer Stephen Marshall was jailed for life in 2010 for killing his landlord Jeffrey Howe and scattering his dismembered body parts across two counties. But which notorious north London crime family – AKA the Clerkenwell Crime Syndicate – did Marshall also claim to have dismembered bodies for?

10. The 1995 murders of three drug dealers in Rettendon, Essex – better known as the 'Range Rover Murders' – were rumoured to be linked to the widely publicised death of which teenager who died weeks earlier after taking ecstasy?

ANSWERS

1. c)   The Blind Beggar. Ronnie was jailed for life three years later.

2. a)   Jack McVitie. Reggie planned to shoot him but when his gun jammed he stabbed him multiple times instead.

3. Richardson. George Cornell had been part of the Richardson crew after switching allegiances from the Krays around 1964.

4. Poland.

5. Bobby Cummines.

6. c)   Elephants. They were based in London's Elephant and Castle.

7. *Lock, Stock and Two Smoking Barrels.*

8. Elvis Presley.

9. The Adams family.

10. Leah Betts.

Quiz 40 – Match the Geezers

Which organized crime group of today and yesteryear do we associate with these underworld legends? Pair them up with the list below.

1. Alfred Solomon

2. Billy Kimber

3. Reggie and Ronnie Kray

4. Charles and Wal McDonald

5. 'Mad' Frankie Fraser

6. John Gotti

7. George 'Bugs' Moran

8. Sergei Mikhailov

9. Joseph Massino

10. Satoru Nomura

a) The Elephant and Castle Mob

b) Gambino crime family

c) The Yiddishers

d) The Richardson Gang

e) Solntsevskaya Bratva

f) The Yakuza

g) The Bonanno crime family

h) The Brummagem Boys

i) North Side Gang

j) The Firm

ANSWERS

1. c)

2. h)

3. j)

4. a)

5. d)

6. b)

7. i)

8. e)

9. g)

10. f)

KIDNAP

Here one minute, and the next – gone. Whether they're for a hefty ransom or to satisfy some perverted desire, kidnappings tear lives and relationships apart. In unsolved cases, the years of clinging to hope must be nothing short of agony. Thankfully, among the heartache and bloodshed there have been some rare and remarkable happy endings.

Quiz 41 – Famous Kidnaps, Trivia

1. Who was behind the abduction in 1992 of Stephanie Slater, who was released after eight days in a coffin-like box upon the payment of a £175,000 ransom by her employer?

2. What was Slater's occupation at the time of the kidnapping?

3. What disability did her kidnapper have?

   a) He only had one arm
   b) He was deaf
   c) He had a wooden leg

4. Name the Portuguese fishing town that Madeleine McCann was abducted from in 2007 at the age of three.

5. What nickname did the press give to Madeleine's parents, Kate and Gerry, and the group of parents they were holidaying with?

6. What nickname did the press give to kidnapper and multiple murderer Donald Neilson for the black balaclava he wore during post office raids?

   a) The Masked Marauder
   b) The Black Panther
   c) The Night Stalker

7. Which iconic silent movie star was 'kidnapped' posthumously from his last resting place near Geneva a year after his death in 1977, with the grave robbers demanding a $600,000-ransom for the return of his corpse?

8. Name the Austrian sentenced to life imprisonment in 2009 for murder, enslavement, rape and incest after keeping his own daughter locked in a cellar prison chamber for twenty-four years and fathering multiple children by her.

9. What did leftist radicals the Symbionese Liberation Army force their newspaper heiress captive Patty Hearst to do after kidnapping her from her Berkeley, California, flat in 1974?

   a) Bomb Wall Street
   b) Gift the family fortune to Fidel Castro
   c) Rob banks at gunpoint

10. How did kidnapper Wolfgang Přiklopil meet his sticky end after abductee Natascha Kampusch escaped from her cellar prison following eight years of captivity?

ANSWERS

1. Michael Sams.

2. Estate agent – Sams posed as a house buyer to kidnap Slater at knifepoint. He was jailed in 1993 for Slater's abduction, and for the murder of a previous victim, Julie Dart. He remains incarcerated to this day.

3. c) He had a wooden leg – and sued the prison service for four thousand pounds when they lost it during a transfer.

4. Praia da Luz.

5. The Tapas Seven. The group met nightly for dinner at the resort's tapas restaurant and were there when Madeleine was abducted from her room nearby.

6. b) The Black Panther.

7. Charlie Chaplin. Police caught up with the crooks and recovered Chaplin's body. His family then had him interred in a concrete grave to prevent a repeat.

8. Josef Fritzl.

9. c) Rob banks. Hearst was captured on CCTV holding up a San Francisco bank. When the FBI caught up with her she claimed she acted under duress, but was found guilty of bank robbery and jailed for seven years. She served three after President Carter commuted her sentenced and was fully pardoned in 2001 by President Clinton.

10. He killed himself by stepping in front of a train. His decapitated corpse was found on a railway line in Vienna.

Quiz 42 – Kidnap Whodunnit

Pair these kidnapping victims to their abductor from the list below.

1. Elizabeth Smart – kidnapped at knifepoint aged fourteen from her home in Salt Lake City, Utah, and held for nine months before she was rescued by police.

2. Steven Sayner – disappeared on his way home from school in Merced, California, at seven years old, only to escape seven years later carrying his abductor's other, five-year-old, victim – Timothy White – on his back.

3. Jaycee Dugard – snatched in 1991 aged eleven, she stayed missing for eighteen years before resurfacing with her captor and the two daughters he had fathered by her.

4. Charles Lindbergh Jr. The son of a famous aviator, he was snatched in 1932 aged just twenty months from the family home in New Jersey. Despite the payment of a ransom, the infant child was later found dead from a blow to the head.

5. Etan Patz – the first child in America to feature in a national milk carton campaign featuring missing kids. He vanished from Manhattan, aged six, as he walked to the school bus stop and was never seen again.

6. Shawn Hornbeck – snatched aged eleven as he cycled to a pal's house near Richwoods, Missouri. He remained missing for four years and was rescued by the FBI in 2007 after his abductor was witnessed kidnapping another child.

7. Carlina White – abducted as a newborn at a mere nineteen days old from Harlem hospital. She was raised to adulthood by her kidnapper and later solved the mystery of her own disappearance when she stumbled on photos of herself as a baby on a missing kids website.

8. Sabine Dardenne – abducted on her way to school aged twelve and kept in her captor's basement. He went on to kidnap another young girl after Dardenne said she wanted a pal to visit. Both girls were rescued by the police six days later.

9. Cleo Smith – just four years old when she was snatched from the family tent in October 2021. She was held captive for three weeks in a locked room with a mattress on the floor.

10. Erica Pratt – this plucky seven-year-old was held captive in an empty house with her hands and feet bound after being snatched off the street in Philadelphia. She gnawed through duct tape and smashed a window to escape.

a) Bruno Hauptmann – a German-born carpenter and burglar who stowed away to America aged twenty-four. He was sentenced to die for his kidnapping crime but went to the chair protesting his innocence.

b) Michael Devlin – pizza shop owner and part-time funeral director's worker. He maintained the falsehood that his victim was his own child. Convicted of kidnapping and child sex offences, he was jailed for four thousand years.

c) Edward Johnson – worked in tandem with getaway driver James Burns and demanded a $150,000 ransom from their victim's family. The plot was foiled and they were both jailed.

d) Brian Mitchell – a pan-handling preacher who claimed to be a prophet of god and dressed in white robes.

e) Terence Kelly – an Aboriginal man who suffered an appalling upbringing and had speech, hearing and developmental issues. He reportedly went looking for handbags to steal while high on drugs, but ended up stealing a child instead.

f) Kenneth Parnell – a convicted child sex offender, he made his victim pose as his own child, claiming a judge had given him custody.

g) Pedro Hernandez – a former store stock clerk, he lured his quarry to the shop basement by promising him a soda and choked him. He was brought to justice almost forty years later after his brother-in-law dobbed him in, and was locked up in 2017.

h) Ann Pettway – suffered several miscarriages and reportedly kidnapped out of desperation to become a mum. She was jailed in 2012 for twelve years and was released in 2021.

i) Marc Paul Alain Dutroux – this former scrap dealer was dealt with leniently for the rape and abduction of multiple young girls in the late eighties, and was out on parole after just three years. He picked up where he left off, eventually kidnapping six girls, two of whom he murdered.

j) Phillip Garrido – a convicted sex offender who had spent eleven years inside for abduction and rape, he was visiting a university campus in Berkeley, California, in 2009 with his adolescent daughters when his unusual behaviour brought him to the attention of authorities.

ANSWERS

1. d)

2. f)

3. j)

4. a)

5. g)

6. b)

7. h)

8. i)

9. e)

10. c)

CULTS

They're hotbeds of coercive control, psychological manipulation and, frequently, sexual abuse, populated by deranged, depraved if, ultimately, charismatic leaders. Some wield so much influence that hundreds of people will follow them to their doom – all fertile territory for the true crime fan.

Quiz 43 – Cults Trivia

1. In which South American country did the Jonestown Massacre take place in 1978, when over nine hundred people died from cyanide poisoning in a combination of murder and suicide at the Peoples Temple Project, set up by preacher Jim Jones?

2. Who was the US congressman sent to investigate the Peoples Temple, only to be shot dead on the runway as he waited to take off for the return trip home?

   a) Leo Ryan
   b) Leigh Till
   c) Luke Hamill

3. Who was the charismatic leader of the Seventh-Day Adventist sect involved in a standoff with the FBI near Waco, Texas, in 1993, which ended in a fire and a tear-gas attack, leaving eighty-two cult members dead?

4. Which domestic terrorist visited the scene of the Waco siege and in 1995 – on the second anniversary of the FBI's tear-gas attack – committed the deadliest act of homegrown terrorism in US history?

5. Thirty-nine members of the Heaven's Gate cult committed mass suicide at a San Diego mansion in 1997, believing death would allow them to ride an alien spacecraft to a higher existence. Where did they think this spacecraft was hiding?

a) In the rings of Saturn
b) On the moon
c) Behind the Hale-Bopp comet

6. What was the name of the suicide cult based on the Knights Templar, best known for the murder-suicide of seventy-four members between 1994–7 in Switzerland, Canada and France?

a) The Knights of Saint Christopher
b) Hermetic Order of the Blue Rose
c) Order of the Solar Temple

7. Name the self-help guru behind the pyramid scheme sex cult NXIVM, jailed for 120 years in 2020 for sex trafficking, racketeering and child pornography.

8. Which US state did the Rajneeshpuram cult relocate to from India in 1981, only to implode four years later when members tried to infect a local town with salmonella and plotted to assassinate the state attorney?

9. What was the name of the cult-like radical Christian group based in Sheffield which used rave music and bikini-clad dancers in its youth-orientated services before collapsing in 1995 amid sex abuse claims?

10. What African country was home to the Movement for the Restoration of the Ten Commandments of God doomsday cult, whose seven hundred followers were locked inside a church and set on fire in 2000 when leaders' predictions of a new millennium apocalypse failed to materialise?

ANSWERS

1. Guyana.

2. a) Leo Ryan. He was shot twenty times. Three journalists and a temple defector were also killed by Jim Jones's 'Red Brigade' security squad.

3. David Koresh.

4. Oklahoma City bomber Timothy McVeigh.

5. c) Behind the Hale-Bopp comet.

6. c) Order of the Solar Temple.

7. Keith Raniere.

8. Oregon.

9. The Nine O'Clock Service.

10. Uganda.

UNSOLVED

Despite the best efforts of law enforcers, dogged detectives and amateur sleuths, some cases just can't be cracked. For the families left behind, it's a lifetime of torment. For the perpetrator – a lifetime of looking over the shoulder.

Quiz 44 – Unsolved UK Crime Trivia

1. What was the fishy name of the supposed house hunter that estate agent Suzy Lamplugh had an appointment with when she vanished in 1986?

2. Name the Greek holiday island where twenty-one-month-old toddler Ben Needham went missing in 1989 with police eventually surmising he died in an accident after wandering away from his grandparents' farm.

3. What long-running policing TV show was Jill Dando presenting before she was executed by a single gunshot to the temple on the doorstep of her home in Fulham in 1999?

4. What name did the police give to the headless, limbless torso of a young Nigerian boy found in the Thames in 2001, who officers believe was the victim of a ritual sacrifice?

5. What nickname has been given to the rapist who terrorised Bath, Somerset, for almost a decade to the year 2000, with seventeen unsolved attacks leading to Britain's most extensive and longest running serial rape inquiry?

6. What fate did the prosecution allege befell missing Blackpool teenager Charlene Downes during the 2007 trial of two takeaway owners accused of her murder?

7. Which serial child killer, who died in prison in 2016, do police believe was behind the 1978 disappearance of Devon newspaper-delivery girl Genette Tate?

8. What south-east Asian country was Welsh backpacker Kirsty Jones in when she was raped and murdered in her guesthouse in 2000?

9. How was private detective Daniel Morgan murdered in the car park of a Sydenham pub in 1987 in a still unsolved case which exposed institutional corruption in the Met police?

10. What was the name of the detective agency Morgan ran with business partner Jonathan Rees?

   a) Sydenham PI
   b) Sleuth South London
   c) Southern Investigations

ANSWERS

1. Mr Kipper.

2. Kos.

3. *Crimewatch*.

4. Adam.

5. The 'Batman Rapist' – he left a baseball cap bearing the Batman logo as he fled one failed attack in 1999.

6. She was supposedly chopped up and turned into kebabs. The trial ended with no verdict and after a retrial was ordered the Crown Prosecution Service offered no evidence against the two accused.

7. Robert Black.

8. Thailand. The crime passed the country's statute of limitations in August 2020, meaning no one will ever be brought to justice.

9. An axe blow to the head.

10. c) Southern Investigations.

Quiz 45 – Unsolved US Crime Trivia

1. Where was the body of six-year-old beauty queen JonBenét Ramsey later found after her family woke to a $118,000 ransom note on Boxing Day 1990?

2. What is the astrological pseudonym of the unidentified serial killer thought to have murdered at least five people in the San Francisco Bay area between 1968–9?

3. What nickname is twenty-two-year-old Hollywood hopeful Elizabeth Short, found cut in half at the waist in Los Angeles, 1947, better known by?

4. What deadly substance were Tylenol painkiller capsules poisoned with in Chicago in 1982, causing the unsolved deaths of seven victims?

5. How did the mystery skyjacker who took control of a Boeing 727 to secure a $200,000 ransom flee the scene of his crime?

6. Name the West Coast hip-hop legend who died four days after being gunned down in Las Vegas in 1996 by a mystery shooter in a white Cadillac.

7. And what was the name of his East Coast rival, shot and killed in a drive-by just months later in what some have hypothesised was an act of revenge?

8. Where did officers carrying out a routine check on the home of elderly Houston couple Fred and Edwina Rogers discover their bodies?

   a) In the fridge
   b) On a bonfire in the garden
   c) Half-buried in fresh concrete

9. Name the *Superman* actor whose death by a single gunshot wound to the head is the subject of enduring rumours that he was the victim of a mob-orchestrated hit – despite an official suicide ruling.

10. Where in 1982 did Alaska's biggest-ever mass murder take place?

    a) On a fishing boat
    b) On an oil rig
    c) On a ski lift

ANSWERS

1. In the cellar of the family home in Boulder, Colorado. No one has been brought to justice.

2. The Zodiac Killer. He continued to taunt police with letters and coded messages sent to newspapers until 1974, and claimed to be behind thirty-seven murders.

3. Black Dahlia.

4. Cyanide.

5. Equipped with a parachute, he jumped from the plane mid-flight, carrying his ransom booty.

6. Tupac Shakur.

7. Christopher Wallace, AKA 'Notorious B.I.G.', AKA 'Biggie Smalls'.

8. a) In the fridge. The officers thought at first it was stacked with cuts of meat – until they noticed the head in the vegetable drawer.

9. George Reeves.

10. a) On a fishing boat named *The Investor*. Boat captain Mark Coulthurst, his wife, two children and four deckhands were all shot dead before the vessel was set ablaze.

Quiz 46 – Unsolved UK Crime Trivia, Round 2

1. Everyone knows the British peer who vanished off the face of the Earth after his kids' nanny was battered to death as Lord Lucan, but what is his actual name?

2. What nickname was Lucan known to friends by?

   a) Lucky   b) Bond   c) The Lieutenant

3. What unusual circumstances were the body of GCHQ analyst and spy Gareth Williams found in at a London safe house in 2010, leading to claims he was murdered?

4. Which UK security service was Gareth working for at the time of his death?

5. How were the scattered remains of twenty-five-year-old Melanie Hall, who vanished from Bath in 1996, found thirteen years later in 2009?

6. What nickname did the press give the unknown killer of six women found strangled and naked in or near the River Thames in west London between 1964–5?

7. Bunny girl and centrefold model Eve Stratford was found murdered in her Leyton flat in 1975 with her throat cut from ear to ear. Which notorious, old school celebrity haunt based in Mayfair did Eve waitress at?

8. Which legendary Glasgow music and dance venue did the – as yet unidentified serial killer – known as Bible John meet all three of his victims in during the late 1960s?

9. In which Kenyan safari reserve was the burned and dismembered corpse of British wildlife photographer Julie Ward found in September 1988?

10. Name the York-based chef who was last seen after leaving the city's Goodricke College in March 2009 in a still-unsolved case of suspected murder.

ANSWERS

1. Richard Bingham.

2. a) Lucky. The keen Aston Martin driver was considered for the role of James Bond – before it was given instead to Sean Connery.

3. His decomposing remains were found padlocked inside a red holdall which had been placed in his bath. An inquest found his death was likely to be 'criminally meditated'. Scotland Yard disagreed and said it was most likely an accident.

4. MI6.

5. Partial remains including a thigh bone and her skull were found in a plastic bag beside the M5 in Gloucestershire. More remains were found in an adjacent field. The case is still unsolved.

6. Jack the Stripper. The case is known as the Hammersmith nude murders.

7. The Playboy club. Eve's murder has been linked by DNA to a second unsolved killing six months later, that of Lynne Weedon in Hounslow on the other side of London.

8. The Barrowland Ballroom.

9. Masai Mara.

10. Claudia Lawrence.

MISCARRIAGES OF JUSTICE

Miscarriages of justice are mercifully rare, but occasionally the police do get it wrong – and the consequences can be devastating, if not fatal. These cases show it could happen to anyone. Even you.

Quiz 47 – UK Miscarriages of Justice, Trivia

1. Who wrongfully spent a year in custody accused of the murder of Rachel Nickell on Wimbledon Common in 1992 after he was ensnared in a heavily criticised Met police honeytrap operation?

   a) Robert Napper
   b) Colin Stagg
   c) Levi Bellfield

2. Whose murder was Barry George jailed for life for in July 2001, only to have his conviction quashed six years later?

3. Police issued a photofit of a bloodstained, white male they suspected of stabbing to death Lynette White in 1988 but then arrested five black and mixed race men for the crime. Three of the men were wrongly convicted and jailed. In which Welsh city did the murder take place?

4. Who was unmasked as Lynette White's real killer and jailed for life in 2003 after concealing his crime for fifteen years?

   a) Jeffrey Gafoor
   b) Joseph Knappen
   c) John Cooper

5. How would evidence of semen on eleven-year-old Rochdale murder victim Lesley Molseed's clothes – which was suppressed at Stefan Kiszko's trial – have exonerated him?

   a) Kiszko was not producing sperm
   b) DNA would have revealed a mismatch
   c) Police would have had to confess to planting it

6. Which British high-street institution was at the centre of a massive miscarriage of justice involving the wrongful convictions of over seven hundred people for theft, fraud and false accounting, when in fact faulty software was to blame?

7. For whose murders was Angela Cannings wrongfully jailed for life in 2002 before her conviction was overturned a year later?

8. Whose amateur sleuthing exonerated Stephen Downing, who served twenty-seven years after being wrongfully convicted of the murder of Wendy Sewell in Bakewell, Derbyshire, in 1973?

   a) His local vicar's
   b) His former geography teacher's
   c) His local newspaper editor's

9. For which IRA bombing – killing twelve people in 1974 – did Judith Ward serve seventeen years of a life sentence, before she was exonerated and freed in 1992?

10. How are Paul Hill, Gerard Conlon, Patrick Armstrong and Carole Richardson, who served fifteen years for IRA bombings they didn't commit, better known?

ANSWERS

1. b) Colin Stagg. The case was thrown out in 1994 when it eventually reached the Old Bailey. Multiple murderer and rapist Robert Napper was already being held in Broadmoor when he admitted killing Rachel in 2008, pleading guilty to manslaughter on the grounds of diminished responsibility.

2. Jill Dando. George was sent for retrial in 2008 and was found not guilty.

3. Cardiff. The convicted men became known as the Cardiff Three. Their conviction was quashed by the Court of Appeal in 1992.

4. a) Jeffrey Gafoor. He was jailed for life with a minimum tariff of thirteen years – a term shorter than two of the three men wrongfully jailed.

5. a) Kizsko was taking medication which meant his semen did not contain sperm, but the sample on Lesley's clothes did. He served sixteen years in prison and died a mentally and emotionally broken man less than two years after his release. Comic-book shop owner Ronald Castree was finally revealed as the real killer – and caged – in 2007, almost thirty years after committing the crime.

6. The Post Office.

7. Those of her sons, Jason and Matthew, aged seven weeks and eighteen weeks respectively. The Court of Appeal agreed they were not smothered but were victims of cot death.

8. c) Crusading newspaper editor Don Hale exposed the injustice, receiving death threats in the process. Downing was freed in 2001. Wendy's murder remains unsolved.

9. The M62 coach bombing.

10. The Guildford Four.

Quiz 48 – US Miscarriages of Justice, Trivia

1. Which American city's corrupt Gun Trace Task Force was dismantled after thirteen rogue officers were charged in 2017 and convicted of offences including racketeering, robbery, selling seized drugs and falsifying records, leading to some eight hundred tainted cases being dropped?

2. Name the groundbreaking investigative true crime podcast which featured the plight of Adnan Syed, who spent more than twenty years in prison for the murder of his ex-girlfriend Hae Min Lee before his conviction was quashed in 2022.

3. Neurosurgeon Sam Sheppard was convicted in 1954 of murdering his pregnant wife, but was acquitted at a second trial after more than ten years in prison. Which Hollywood movie, with Harrison Ford in the lead as Dr Richard Kimble, did the Sheppard case inspire?

4. How are the five young men wrongfully convicted in 1989 over the rape and assault of a New York jogger better known?

5. Name the real estate mogul and future US president who called for the reinstatement of the death penalty in New York following these five wrongful convictions.

6. How old was George Stinney Jr when he was put to death by electric chair in 1944 for the murders of two children – crimes he did not commit – making him the youngest in twentieth-century America to be executed?

   a) 10
   b) 14
   c) 17

7. How did Stinney's executioners overcome the problem of his short stature when his death penalty was carried out?

8. Name the British au pair convicted in Massachusetts in 1997 of the second-degree murder of Matthew Eappen, the baby in her care, only to be freed eleven days later when a judge reduced the charge to involuntary manslaughter, saying the conviction had been a 'miscarriage of justice'.

9. Which controversial procedure – a factor in multiple cases of wrongful conviction across the US – is banned for use by employers for screening potential employees, but can still be used in some states to provide evidence for criminal trials?

    a) An identity parade
    b) A background check
    c) A lie detector test

10. How many people sentenced to die in the US have subsequently been exonerated and freed since the early 1970s?

    a) 25+
    b) 100+
    c) 190+

ANSWERS

1. Baltimore's.

2. *Serial.*

3. *Fugitive.*

4. The Central Park Five. They served between five and twelve years in prison but were exonerated in 2002 when serial rapist Matias Reyes confessed to the crime.

5. Donald Trump. He has refused to apologise for his comments.

6. b) He was fourteen. An all-white jury took ten minutes to find the black boy guilty after a trial lasting just two-and-a-half hours. He was exonerated posthumously in 2014.

7. They had him sit on a bible as a booster seat.

8. Louise Woodward. Her sentence was reduced from life to time served on remand and she was released.

9. c) The polygraph, or lie detector test.

10. c) The figure is 190-plus. No one knows exactly how many wrongly convicted prisoners have been executed, but a 2014 study found that around 4 per cent of defendants given the death penalty are innocent.

GOOD COP, BAD COP

Crime fighting heroes come in many guises, and most of them we never even get to hear about. It's all part of the job, right? The rotten apples, though, that's a different story – and there's nothing quite as rotten as a bent cop.

Quiz 49 – Good Cops Trivia

1. In 1990, flying squad detective Jack Slipper, AKA Slipper of the Yard, won £50,000 in damages from the BBC for its libellous portrayal of his efforts to extradite which on-the-run crook?

2. What crime fighting tool still in use today is the late Scotland Yard officer Fred Cherrill credited with creating in 1930?

   a) Photofit reconstruction
   b) Blood spatter pattern analysis
   c) The fingerprint system

3. Detective Sergeant Nick Bailey began investigating an odd case of two people found slumped on a bench in Salisbury, Wiltshire, in 2018 – but two days later his sleuthing landed him in hospital fighting for his life. Why?

4. Which spree-killer gunman blasted tragic PC David Rathband in the face with a shotgun in 2010, leaving him permanently blinded and leading to his suicide twenty months later?

5. Ex-flying squad detective and police corruption whistleblower Jackie Malton provided the real-life inspiration for which famously tenacious fictional TV sleuth?

6. Besides a Glock pistol, what piece of ordnance did multiple killer Dale Cregan use when he murdered female PCs Fiona Bone and Nicola Hughes in Manchester in 2012?

7. Name the police colleague of 1984 embassy shooting victim Yvonne Fletcher who waged a thirty-seven-year campaign to identify her killer, culminating in a high court ruling, holding former Gadaffi aide Ibrahim Mabrouk jointly liable.

8. Which controversial and openly gay, high-ranking officer piloted a softly-softly approach to cannabis possession in 2001 during his tenure as Lambeth police chief where users were let off with a warning?

9. London's first organised police force was created in 1829 by Home Secretary Sir Robert Peel, leading to officers being known as 'bobbies'. What alternative nickname were they given?

10. Which serial killer – convicted in two separate cases in 2008 and 2011 of three murders – is Met police detective Colin Sutton best known for bringing to justice?

ANSWERS

1. Great Train robber Ronnie Biggs.

2. c) He built up a database of a million fingerprints and was considered the world's greatest fingerprint expert of his time.

3. He was poisoned with the Novichok nerve agent after touching the substance smeared on the door handle of Russian assassination target Sergei Skripal.

4. Raoul Moat. PC Rathband never came to terms with his disability and hanged himself in 2012.

5. Jane Tennison, played by Helen Mirren in *Prime Suspect*.

6. A hand grenade. Cregan was wanted for two gangland murders when he lured the two officers into a trap. He will die behind bars after being given a whole-life sentence for his crimes.

7. John Murray.

8. Brian Paddick.

9. Peelers.

10. Levi Bellfield.

Quiz 50 – Bad Cops Trivia, US Edition

1. In what must be the ultimate case of *schadenfreude*, what firearm mishap during the shooting of one of his multiple victims led to the capture of Miami-based ex-cop turned serial killer Manuel Pardo Jr?

2. The 1992 acquittal and no verdict in the case of four LAPD officers accused of police brutality touched off the Los Angeles riots. Who had been on the receiving end of their alleged thuggery the year before?

3. Whose death at the hands of Minneapolis cop Derek Chauvin is commemorated with a period of silence lasting eight minutes and forty-six seconds?

4. Which city police department is associated with late detective Jon Burge, accused of running a crew of rogue cops who extracted false confessions using torture?

   a) Chicago PD
   b) New York PD
   c) Seattle PD

5. Which controversial West Coast hip-hop label reportedly hired moonlighting LAPD cops from its infamous 'Rampart' gangs unit, which imploded in the early 2000s amid accusations that officers stole and sold drugs, robbed banks and planted evidence?

6. Which 2005 natural disaster had recently ravaged New Orleans when police shot dead two unarmed, innocent civilians at the city's Danziger Bridge?

7. Which American coastal city police department fired or suspended some 10 per cent of its officers in the late eighties over a drug scandal involving officers robbing dealers for their cocaine and cash?

   a) San Diego PD
   b) Miami PD
   c) Philadelphia PD

8. Systemic corruption and vice racketeering in the New York PD was exposed in the seventies by whistleblowing plainclothes detective Frank Serpico. Which screen icon played him in a 1973 movie which took his surname as its title?

9. Ex-LAPD cop Christopher Dorner killed four people in a nine-day vendetta against law enforcers and their families in 2013, before he barricaded himself in a mountain cabin and shot himself in the head. In which Californian ski resort was the cabin located?

   a) Big Bear
   b) Dodge Ridge
   c) Alta Sierra

10. New Orleans PD officer Antoinette Frank was convicted in 1995 of murdering three in cold blood in a botched robbery at a Vietnamese restaurant. Where is she now?

ANSWERS

1. He shot himself in the foot. The recovered bullet matched those recovered from previous victims. He was convicted of nine murders and died by lethal injection in 2012.

2. Rodney King. Three officers were acquitted of using excessive force and the jury failed to reach a verdict on the fourth. They were all tried again in a federal civil rights case in 1993, with two officers being found guilty and jailed, and two acquitted.

3. George Floyd's. Eight minutes, forty-six seconds is the length of time Chauvin knelt on Floyd's neck. He was jailed for over twenty-two years with the judge noting Chauvin had treated Floyd with 'particular cruelty'.

4. a) Chicago PD. Burge was fired in 1993 but escaped prosecution for his actions as the statute of limitations had passed. However, he was jailed for perjury in 2012 after a jury found he had lied in a civil suit against him alleging torture.

5. Death Row Records.

6. Hurricane Katrina.

7. b) Miami.

8. Al Pacino.

9. a) Big Bear.

10. At the time of writing, she is the only woman on death row in the state of Louisiana.

Quiz 51 – Bad Cops Trivia, UK Edition

1. Which elite armed division did killer Met police officer Wayne Couzens serve in?

   a) Counter Terrorist Specialist Firearms Unit
   b) Specialist Firearms Command
   c) Parliamentary and Diplomatic Protection

2. Name the fellow officer who served in the same division and who was given thirty-six life sentences in 2023 for violent sexual offending stretching over two decades, including almost fifty rapes against twelve women.

3. Which seminal American crime drama series inspired corrupt Met police officer Mesut Karakas, jailed in 2010 for plotting to kidnap a bank manager in the hope of extorting £100,000?

4. Which TV star was jailed in 1998 for scheming with corrupt Liverpool cop Elmore Davies to wreck the trial of an associate of jailed drug lord Curtis Warren?

   a) Russ Abbott
   b) Warrior from Gladiators AKA Mike Ahearne
   c) Michael Barrymore

5. In 2021, PC Benjamin Monk was jailed for eight years for manslaughter after tasering former Aston Villa striker Dalian Atkinson and kicking him in the head in an incident in Telford, Shropshire. Which police force did Monk serve with?

   a) West Midlands
   b) Dyfed Powys
   c) West Mercia

6. How did Met police officers Deniz Jaffer and Jamie Lewis abuse their role guarding the scene of a double murder in 2020, leading to the two cops being jailed for two years and nine months?

7. Name the former Met police chief who in 2005 was head of the force's counter-terrorism unit when its officers shot and killed Brazilian electrician Jean Charles de Menezes in a fatal case of mistaken identity.

8. Which London tube station was Menezes killed at?

   a) Stockwell
   b) Brixton
   c) Bayswater

9. How are Winston Trew, Sterling Christie, George Griffiths and Constantine Boucher – wrongly jailed in 1972 for bag-snatching on the London underground after being fitted up by bent cop Derek Ridgewell – better known?

   a) The 'Oval Four'
   b) The 'Stockwell Four'
   c) The 'Paddington Four'

10. For whose killing were the so-called 'Bridgewater Four' wrongly jailed for in 1979 after being framed by corrupt West Midlands police detective John Perkins, who boasted of using his fists as a 'truth drug'?

ANSWERS

1. c) The Parliamentary and Diplomatic Protection Unit.

2. David Carrick.

3. *The Wire*. A bug placed in Karakas's car recorded him discussing tips on dodging detection gleaned from the hit show.

4. b) Warrior from *Gladiators* – AKA Mike Ahearne. He got fifteen months, Davies was jailed for five years.

5. c) West Mercia.

6. They took photos of the bodies of sisters Bibaa Henry and Nicole Smallman and passed them around friends in a WhatsApp group.

7. Cressida Dick.

8. a) Stockwell.

9. a) The 'Oval Four'. They were exonerated in 2019 after decades of campaigning. Ridgewell had died in prison in 1982 while serving seven years for theft from mailbags.

10. Paperboy Carl Bridgewater. Three of the four were jailed for life for murder and served almost two decades before their convictions were quashed. The fourth man – Patrick Molloy – died two years into a twelve-year sentence for manslaughter.

FAMOUS TRIALS

The high drama of the courtroom has made for plenty of scene-stealing moments over the years, and occasionally the impact of a big trial reverberates down the years long after its protagonists have hung up their wigs and gowns.

Quiz 52 – Trials Trivia

1. Whose televised, eight-month trial extravaganza – beginning in January 1995 – was famously preceded six months earlier by a sixty-mile-an-hour slow-speed police chase through Los Angeles and Orange County?

2. What was the name of the report that led to Bill Clinton being impeached for 'high crimes and misdemeanours' in connection with the Monica Lewinsky scandal?

   a) The Jones Report
   b) The Tripp Report
   c) The Starr Report

3. The trial of American novelist Michael Petersen for the suspected murder of his wife, Kathleen, was followed in an acclaimed documentary by French director Jean-Xavier de Lestrade. Where was Kathleen found dead?

4. How did Nazi leader Hermann Göring spend his last night in his prison cell after being convicted of war crimes at the Nuremberg Trials and sentenced to death by hanging?

5. What name is given to the court proceedings which took place in colonial Massachusetts between 1692 and 1693 resulting in twenty executions for practising the 'devil's magic'?

6. Name the accused murderer immortalised in a nursery rhyme after she was acquitted at an 1892 show trial of axing her father and stepmother to death in Fall River, Massachusetts.

7. What seismic change to the criminal justice system was brought about by the wrongful conviction by mistaken identity of Adolf Beck on fraud charges at the Old Bailey in 1896?

   a) The Court of Criminal Appeal was created
   b) Scotland Yard started a fingerprint database
   c) Identity parades were introduced

8. The repeal of which law meant that Gary Dobson could be retried for the murder of Stephen Lawrence after his acquittal in a private prosecution brought by the victim's parents in 1996?

9. The murder of which British exchange student in Perugia, Italy, in 2007 resulted in an eight-year to-and-fro through the courts for suspects Amanda Knox and boyfriend Raffaele Sollecito, before the pair were cleared once and for all in 2015?

10. The 1970–71 'Manson Family' murder trial was the longest-running in American legal history at the time, stretching over nine-and-a-half months and concluding with all four defendants being sentenced to death. How, by the skin of their teeth, did they avoid being executed?

    a) The death penalty was abolished in California the following year
    b) The executioner was a Manson fan and refused to carry out the sentence
    c) The victims' families pleaded with the court for clemency

ANSWERS

1. OJ Simpson's. He was – controversially – acquitted of the murders of ex-wife Nicole Simpson and her friend Ronald Goldman. At a civil trial the following year he was sued by the victims' families and found responsible for the deaths. The families were awarded $33.5 million in damages.

2. c) The Starr Report, by judge Kenneth Starr. At a senate trial in 1999 Clinton was acquitted on both articles of impeachment – lying under oath to a federal grand jury and obstructing justice.

3. At the bottom of the staircase in the family home. The documentary was called . . . *The Staircase*. Peterson was convicted of murder and jailed for life in 2003. He was released in 2011 and granted a new trial, but in 2017 entered an Alford plea to a reduced charge of manslaughter. He was sentenced to time served. An Alford plea is a guilty plea entered because sufficient evidence exists for conviction, but the defendant asserts his or her innocence.

4. Committing suicide with a cyanide capsule.

5. The 'Salem Witch Trials'.

6. Lizzie Borden.

7. a) Until Beck's case, there was no appeal court. Beck was pardoned by the king in 1904.

8. The double jeopardy law – meaning that no one could be tried for the same crime twice. Dobson was found guilty of murder at his second trial in January 2012, alongside co-accused David Norris. The pair were jailed for life.

9. Meredith Kercher.

10. a) The California Supreme Court ruled in 1972 that the death penalty was unconstitutional and the death sentences were commuted to life in jail. California did, however, reinstate the death penalty a few months later.

PRISONS

Some prisons earn reputations as notorious as their inmates, but you know what they say – if you can't do the time, don't do the crime.

Quiz 53 – Prisons Trivia

1. Name the jailed militant who was elected to the House of Commons as an MP in 1981 whilst serving fourteen years for weapons charges.

2. In 1990, which prison was the scene of a twenty-five-day riot which sparked widespread unrest in jails across the UK and ultimately led to a reform of the prison system?

3. Which literary great spent two years in Reading Gaol and famously wrote a poem about the experience following his release in 1897?

   a) Bram Stoker
   b) George Bernard Shaw
   c) Oscar Wilde

4. Other than Ronnie Biggs, which member of the Great Train Robbery gang managed to escape prison?

5. In 1983, thirty-eight IRA inmates broke out of an 'escape-proof' prison in what is still the biggest jailbreak in UK history. Which prison did they flee?

6. In the same jail, how many republicans died in the 1981 hunger strike protesting the British government's refusal to recognise them as political prisoners?

7. Where is the UK's largest prison, HMP Berwyn, located?

8. By what nickname were the men jailed at Wandsworth prison for refusing to fight in World War I known?

9. Hundreds of members of which activist women's group were locked up at Holloway in the early 1900s, with some taking part in hunger strikes in protest?

10. What nickname has been given to HMP Wakefield, the high security prison housing some of the UK's most notorious killers and sex offenders?

ANSWERS

1. Bobby Sands.

2. Strangeways. A public inquiry later condemned prison conditions as intolerable and reforms ended the practice of 'slopping out' toilets while introducing more visits and phone calls.

3. c) Oscar Wilde. He was jailed for 'gross indecency' with other men and later wrote *The Ballad of Reading Gaol,* narrating the execution of a fellow prisoner.

4. Charlie Wilson. He was the crew's treasurer, in charge of dividing up the loot, and was sprung from Winson Green Prison by accomplices, remaining at large for four years.

5. The Maze prison, near Belfast.

6. Ten.

7. Wrexham, North Wales.

8. 'Conchies', or conscientious objectors.

9. The Suffragettes.

10. Monster Mansion.

Quiz 54 – Prison Anagrams

Rearrange the following into the names of the some of the world's most notorious lock-ups.

1. Talc Zara, USA

2. Scour womb words, UK

3. Airless drink, USA

4. Hue retreat, USA

5. Dial LSD veins, French Guiana

6. Ann gawk gb, Thailand

7. Greasy wants, UK

8. Ah Woolly, UK

9. Kale sandpit, Russia

10. Gigs inns, USA

ANSWERS

1. Alcatraz.

2. Wormwood Scrubs.

3. Rikers Island.

4. Terre Haute.

5. Devil's Island.

6. Bang Kwang.

7. Strangeways.

8. Holloway.

9. Petak Island.

10. Sing Sing.

Quiz 55 – Great Escapes

Pair the lag with the jail they escaped from from the list below.

1. Richard Matt and David Sweat – bashed holes in the walls of their cells to gain access to the prison's utility areas before cutting a hole in a pipe and escaping through the sewers.

2. Richard McNair – mailed himself out of the prison, by hiding among a pallet of mailbags which were transported to a storage warehouse nearby. When the coast was clear, he fled to freedom.

3. Choi Gap-Bok – the yoga master smeared himself in body lotion and, like a human octopus, manipulated his super-flexible body through a food slot in the base of his cell wall.

4. Joaquín 'El Chapo' Guzmán – climbed down a shaft below the shower in his cell into a complex tunnel system dug out by accomplices and rode a motorbike all the way to a safe house.

5. John Killick – had his girlfriend hijack a helicopter at gunpoint. It flew into the prison yard and picked him up, escaping in a hail of bullets.

6. Ted Bundy – shed 16kg to squeeze through a grate in the ceiling of his cell and gain access to an empty prison officers' room nearby. He helped himself to some clothes from a locker and walked out the front door.

7. Andrew Rodger, Keith Rose and Matthew Williams – memorised the shape of a prison master key and made one of their own, as well as a ladder and a gun. They used the key to leave via a back door and the ladder to scale the perimeter fence.

8. John Massey – hid in a prison gym before climbing onto the roof and scaling the outside wall with rope fashioned from netting.

9. Nessan Quinlivan and Pearse McAuley – one of the men pulled out a gun hidden in his shoe and the pair fled, firing shots at the guards. They blasted one guard in the leg, stole his car and sped away.

10. John Gerard – sentenced to die for preaching his Catholic beliefs, the Jesuit priest wrote to allies on the outside using invisible ink made from orange juice. They rowed a boat to the walls of his prison and he climbed down on a rope to flee.

a) Altiplano maximum security prison, Mexico.

b) Garfield County Jail, Colorado.

c) Brixton Prison, London.

d) United States Penitentiary, Pollock, Louisiana.

e) Clinton Correctional Facility, Dannemora, USA.

f) Pentonville Prison, London.

g) The Tower of London.

h) Daegu city police holding cell, South Korea.

i) Parkhurst Prison, Isle of Wight.

j) Silverwater Prison, Sydney, Australia.

ANSWERS

1. e)

2. d)

3. h)

4. a)

5. j)

6. b)

7. i)

8. f)

9. c)

10 g)

HISTORICAL CRIMES

History is full of bizarre crimes – and equally bizarre and barbaric punishments. Take a step back in time with these witches, killers and heretics from years gone by.

Quiz 56 – Historical Crime Trivia

1. What did Scottish serial killers William Burke and William Hare do with the sixteen corpses from their murderous spree in 1800s Edinburgh?

   a) Made haggis from them
   b) Sold them to medical researchers
   c) Dumped them at the gates of Edinburgh Castle

2. How are the twelve women – Alice Nutter being the most famous – who were tried for witchcraft in seventeenth-century Lancashire and Yorkshire collectively known?

3. Which ancient Greek philosopher was sentenced to death by poisoning in 399 BC for 'corrupting the youth of Athens'?

4. Name the famous astronomer who in 1633 was condemned for heresy by the Catholic church and sentenced to house arrest for arguing that the Earth moved around the sun.

5. Which eighties' Scottish pop duo, famous for their hit 'Labour of Love', are named after a thirteenth-century statute which compels members of the public to tackle offenders when the alarm is raised about a crime in progress?

6. How was the heavily romanticised horse thief, murderer, rapist and highwayman Dick Turpin brought to justice after assuming another identity?

   a) An old school friend recognised his handwriting
   b) He was caught riding a stolen horse

c) He fell asleep while poaching deer in Walthamstow Forest

7. Which nineteenth-century serial killer's victims are known as the 'Canonical Five'?

8. Name the judicial body, ostensibly set up to combat heresy in Spain and its colonies, which was responsible for the execution of thousands of people over three centuries from the late 1400s onwards.

9. Guy Fawkes was sentenced to die by the torturous method of being hung, drawn and quartered. How did he cheat his executioner out of the pleasure?

   a) He set himself on fire
   b) He jumped from the gallows ladder and broke his neck
   c) He paid a jail guard to shoot him

10. Seventeeth-century noblewoman Erzsébet – or Elizabeth – Báthory gained infamy for practising sadomasochism, torturing servants and bathing in the blood of slain virgins, notching up a murderous toll stretching into the hundreds. What eastern European country was she from?

ANSWERS

1. b) They sold them to anatomist Robert Knox for dissection.

2. The Pendle Witches. Ten were found guilty and hanged, one was cleared and one died in her cell awaiting trial.

3. Socrates. He carried out his own execution by drinking a cup of hemlock.

4. Galileo Galilei. In 1992 – more than three centuries later – the Vatican admitted he had been right after all.

5. Hue and Cry.

6. a) Turpin was using the name Palmer when he was nabbed for stealing horses. He wrote to a relative from prison and by chance it was spotted in a post office by an old classmate who dobbed him in and collected a handsome reward.

7. Jack the Ripper's.

8. The Spanish Inquisition.

9. b) He jumped – or perhaps slipped, who knows? – from the ladder. Either way he died instantly and was spared the agony of being chopped into pieces.

10. Hungary.

LAWS AND LAWMAKING

The law books throw up their fair share of surprises, and myths abound on what does and doesn't constitute law-breaking.

Quiz 57 – Weird Laws

Decide whether these legal oddities are true or false . . .

1. Carrying planks of wood or even a ladder along the pavement in London, unless you happen to be loading or unloading, is illegal.

2. It's illegal to handle salmon in suspicious circumstances.

3. Wearing fancy dress on Easter Sunday is banned under laws dating back to Tudor times.

4. It's illegal to shake your rug in the street.

5. Whispering in a foreign language while travelling on the London Underground is a no-no under laws introduced during World War II.

6. Putting a stamp upside down on a letter is a criminal offence.

7. It's illegal to hold unlicensed gatherings of more than twenty people in the open air where music consisting of a succession of repetitive beats is being played.

8. Under UK law, pregnant women caught short are legally permitted to urinate in a police officer's helmet.

9. London black cabs are legally required to carry a bale of hay and a bag of oats.

10. Being drunk in a pub is a crime.

ANSWERS

1. True, under the Metropolitan Police Act 1839, you could be fined.

2. Also true. It's an offence under the Salmon Act of 1986.

3. False. However, it is illegal to dress as a police officer or as a member of the armed forces on any day of the year.

4. True, it's another gem from the Metropolitan Police Act 1839.

5. False. We made that one up.

6. False. It's a commonly held myth based on the Treason and Felony Act 1848 which makes it illegal to carry out any act with the intention of deposing the monarch.

7. True. The Criminal Justice and Public Order Act 1994 was the government's hamfisted effort to crack down on raves.

8. False, it's just another myth.

9. False. Drivers of horse-drawn hackney carriages weren't allowed to feed their horses in the street, other than by hay out of their hand or oats in a sack, but there was no legal requirement to carry them in their cab.

10. True. It's forbidden under the Licensing Act 1872. In addition, the Licensing Act 2003 makes it an offence to sell booze to someone who is drunk.

BANNED

Quiz 58 – It's Been Banned . . .

Another true or false round – decide whether the following were ever *really* banned by the statute books.

1. Eating mince pies on Christmas Day.

2. Being a communist.

3. Shooting a Welsh or Scotsman with a longbow.

4. Football.

5. Criticising Henry VIII's marriage.

6. Dying in parliament.

7. Buying booze on election day in the US.

8. Urinating on the rear wheel of your car.

9. Promoting homosexuality.

10. Not practising archery.

ANSWERS

1. True – but only for one year, in 1644, when Christmas Day fell on a day of fasting decreed by law.

2. False, although the Communist Party's mouthpiece, the *Daily Worker*, was banned for eighteen months from January 1941.

3. True. It's never been legal, despite an enduring myth that this is still allowed in law today, as long as you do it from certain locations in Hereford, Chester and York. It's not and trying it could lead to a murder charge.

4. True. First banned in 1314 by King Edward II.

5. True. It was against the law to criticize the King's marriage to Anne Boleyn.

6. False. It's never been illegal and is a myth within a myth – it seems to stem from the belief that dying in parliament would entitle you to an eye-wateringly expensive state funeral. It wouldn't.

7. True. The law dates back to 1882. The last state to repeal it was South Carolina, in 2014.

8. True. It's a myth that having a wee on your back wheel with your right hand on the car is OK. Urinating in public is a no-no under the Public Order Act 1986.

9. True. Under Section 28 of the Local Government Act 1986, brought in by Margaret Thatcher's Tory government, it was illegal, for example, for schools to teach about same sex relationships or carry LGBT books or leaflets. It took until 2003 for the law to be repealed.

10. True. Under sixteenth-century law it was mandatory for men to keep a long bow and maintain their archery skills. The legislation was only repealed in 1960.

Quiz 59 – When Was It Banned?

1. Drink driving – when was the maximum legal limit of 80mg
   alcohol per 100ml of blood imposed?

   a) 1872
   b) 1960
   c) 1967

2. When was cocaine outlawed in the UK?

   a) 1920
   b) 1954
   c) 1971

3. When did it become illegal to possess a knuckleduster?

   a) 1953
   b) 1985
   c) 2021

4. When was the Hunting Act introduced in England and Wales,
   banning fox hunting?

   a) 2001
   b) 2004
   c) 2010

5. What year was driving without a seatbelt banned?

   a) 1964
   b) 1983
   c) 1991

6. When did the Race Relations Act, outlawing racial discrimination,
   come in?

   a) 1965
   b) 1972
   c) 1979

7. When was the so-called 'sus-law', which allowed police officers to stop and search anyone on the basis of suspicion alone, finally abolished following criticism it was being unfairly deployed to harass black communities?

    a) 1969
    b) 1974
    c) 1981

8. When did the Computer Misuse Act make computer hacking a crime?

    a) 1990
    b) 1993
    c) 1999

9. What year was smoking in enclosed public places banned in England, Wales and Northern Ireland?

    a) 2006
    b) 2007
    c) 2008

10. When did a change in the law abolish the death penalty for the offence of murder in England, Scotland and Wales, effectively ending its use as a punishment?

    a) 1965
    b) 1972
    c) 1998

ANSWERS

1. c) 1967. However, it was already illegal to be in charge of a motor vehicle while unfit through drink or drugs thanks to the 1960 Road Traffic Act.

2. a) 1920.

3. c) As of 2021 it's illegal to have a knuckleduster even in the home. Before then it was an offence to carry one in public.

4. b) 2004. Scotland banned the practice in 2002.

5. b) 1983. It also became mandatory for front-seat passengers to wear a seatbelt.

6. a) 1965.

7. c) 1981.

8. a) 1990.

9. b) 2007.

10. a) 1965.

WHAT'S YOUR POISON?

Poison has been used to kill and maim since ancient times, but things don't always go to plan . . .

Quiz 60 – Poisoners Trivia

1. Globe-trotting poisoner Thomas Cream killed up to ten people across three different countries and was hanged in London in 1892. Which serial killer did Cream reportedly confess to being as the gallows trapdoor opened and he plummeted to his death?

2. Who did American poisoner Heidi Littlefield rope in as an accomplice to help kill her ex, Francis Kelley, with fentanyl-laced oatmeal in 2022, earning herself a whopping 115 years in jail?

   a) Her mum
   b) Her daughter
   c) Her drug dealer

3. In a quintessentially British act of poisoning, what did 'St Albans Poisoner' Graham Young lace with thallium to kill two work colleagues in 1971?

4. American emergency doctor Deborah Green ground up castor beans and fed them to her husband to poison him with which potent toxin in 1995?

5. What dish did spurned Lakhvir Kaur Singh spice up with the deadly herb aconite to murder her lover Lakhvinder Cheema?

6. To what end did married doctor Edward Erin attempt to poison his lover Bella Prowse after getting her pregnant in a fling that began at a work Christmas party?

7. How is the American homeopath hanged at Pentonville prison in 1910 for poisoning and dismembering his wife Cora colloquially known?

8. Why did Viktoria Nasyrova feed her friend Olga Tsvyk sedative-laced cheesecake in New York in 2016?

    a) To steal her cat
    b) To steal her husband
    c) To steal her identity

9. Where did Australian murderer Rebecca Payne hide the body of her abusive husband after poisoning him with crushed temazepam tablets in home-made biscuits?

    a) Down a well
    b) In a chimney
    c) In a chest freezer

10. Which celebrated drug world crime drama was alleged to have inspired lovestruck Kuntal Patel to acquire a ricin-like toxin, abrin, which she was accused of giving to her 'controlling' mother, Meena?

ANSWERS

1. Jack the Ripper. His executioner claimed Cream said the words, 'I am Jack . . .' but the sentence was cut short by the noose tightening around his neck. Records suggest he was in prison in the States when the Ripper was active.

2. b) Her daughter, Logan Runyon. She testified against her mum and got twenty-six years for conspiracy to commit murder.

3. Their tea.

4. Ricin. Michael survived the attempt. Green also burned down the family home and killed two of the couple's three children.

5. Chicken curry. Singh was jailed for life in 2010.

6. To cause a miscarriage. Prowse noticed her drinks had been tampered with and alerted police. Erin was convicted of two counts of attempted poisoning and jailed for six years.

7. Dr Crippen, AKA Hawley Harvey Crippen. Cora's torso was found buried under the basement of their home.

8. c) Her identity. The two women looked alike and Nasyrova feared being sent back to her Russian homeland where she was wanted for murder. Tsvyk survived the attempt on her life.

9. c) In the freezer. Payne endured years of abuse and was jailed in 2023 for sixteen years in a case which the judge said deserved to be shown mercy.

10. *Breaking Bad*. Londoner Patel was cleared of attempted murder in 2014 but convicted of acquiring a biological agent or toxin and jailed for three years, becoming the first to be sentenced under the Biological Weapons Act 1974.

EXECUTIONS

And so to the end. For some, the *very* end. There was a time when even the most banal of crimes could lead to a date with the executioner. Even today, in some nations, the ultimate punishment remains a staple of law enforcement.

Quiz 61 – How Did They Go?

Pair these famous execution victims with the method that sent them on their final journey from the list below.

1. Ted Bundy, US. Serial killer, rapist and kidnapper.

2. Peter Allen, UK. Murderer.

3. Henri Désiré Landru, France. Serial killer known as the 'Bluebeard of Gambais'.

4. John Wayne Gacy, US. Serial killer and sex offender.

5. Ronnie Lee Gardner, US. Killed a man while trying to escape from a courthouse.

6. Joan of Arc, France. Convicted of heresy.

7. Hadj Mohammed Mesfewi, Morocco. Serial killer.

8. Liu Jin, China. Accused of treason against a Ming dynasty emperor.

9. Barbara Graham, US. Committed murder during a botched robbery.

10. William Wallace, UK. Convicted of treason for leading the fight for Scottish independence.

a) Hanged

b) Gas chamber

c) Being 'walled up' – interred alive in a brick wall

d) Electric chair

e) Burnt at the stake

f) *Lingchi*, or 'death by a thousand cuts'

g) Hanged, drawn and quartered

h) Lethal injection

i) Firing squad

j) Guillotine

ANSWERS

1. d)

2. a)

3. j)

4. h)

5. i)

6. e)

7. c)

8. f)

9. b)

10. g)

Quiz 62 – Executions and Executioners, Trivia

1. The world's longest-serving death row inmate was in which country?

2. What name is given to the method of hanging introduced in nineteenth-century England which calculates – based on the weight of the condemned – the distance they need to fall to break their neck and cause instantaneous death?

3. What is the name of the site near the modern-day Marble Arch which was the scene of public executions stretching over six centuries?

4. Which global superpower is thought to carry out the highest number of executions annually?

5. Teenager Derek Bentley was hanged in 1953 for the joint enterprise murder of a policeman committed during a bungled burglary. What ambiguous and fate-sealing command did he famously give to his gun-toting accomplice when he was challenged by another officer to surrender his weapon?

6. How many American GIs were executed at Shepton Mallet prison over the space of two-and-a-half years for rapes and murders committed during their time stationed in Britain during World War II?

    a) 18   b) 27   c) 36

7. What nickname was the electric chair used in Texas for forty years between 1924–64 known by?

8. In 1982, American Charlie Brooks Jr became the first in the world to be executed by what method?

9. Which feted, globe-trotting British hangman travelled to Europe to execute some two hundred Nazi war criminals in batches at Germany's Hamelin prison?

10. In which country is British drug mule Lindsay Sandiford awaiting death by firing squad following her 2012 conviction for smuggling almost 5kg of cocaine?

ANSWERS

1. Iwao Hakamada was from Japan and spent forty-five years awaiting execution in that country before his 'temporary release' in 2014. He was granted a retrial for the murder of a family of four almost six decades previously.

2. The long drop.

3. Tyburn. By the late sixteenth century it was home to the 'Tyburn Tree', a triangular gallows structure from which as many as twenty-four prisoners were hanged at a time.

4. China. Official figures are a state secret, but Amnesty International estimates the number to be in the thousands. Iran usually tops the charity's official report.

5. 'Let him have it.' Forty years after he was hanged, Bentley was given a royal pardon for his death sentence.

6. a) Eighteen. All but two – who faced the firing squad – were hanged. GIs were responsible for twenty-six murders and almost 130 rapes in the three years between their arrival and the conclusion of the war.

7. 'Old Sparky'.

8. Lethal injection.

9. Albert Pierrepoint.

10. Bali, Indonesia.